If you were SUDDENLY ALONE, could you wake up in the morning; operate effectively throughout the day as you performed the activities of daily living; retire self-assured at night; and repeat that process in the weeks, months, and years to come?

Could you today, without help from anyone, put your hands on all of your financial records, legal documents, personal identification cards, insurance policies, medical records, prescriptions, computer logins and passwords?

Have you thought about what you will do or where you will live if you become incapacitated?

Have you told anyone your wishes upon death?

Are you doing everything you can to take care of yourself and live a healthy lifestyle?

If you answered "YES" to all of the above questions, Congratulations.

If you answered "NO" to any or all of the above questions, Why?

> You do not have all the information needed at your fingertips.
> You do not know what you do not know.
> Someone else has managed all or most of your affairs for you until now…and now you are all alone.

Have you thought about how a comprehensive "Personal Operating Manual" could enable you to answer the above questions "YES"?

This book will help you to develop such a manual.

Suddenly ALONE

A Practical Guide to Prepare Yourself and Your
Loved Ones for When You Are Suddenly Alone

KEN AND DONNA WRIGHT

authorHOUSE®

AuthorHouse™
1663 Liberty Drive
Bloomington, IN 47403
www.authorhouse.com
Phone: 1 (800) 839-8640

Published by AuthorHouse 07/08/2016

ISBN: 978-1-5246-0533-9 (sc)
ISBN: 978-1-5246-0532-2 (e)

<u>DEDICATION</u>

This book is dedicated to the memory of
Blair Torbert Lake Sigler and
Raymond DeHart Sigler, Jr.
who were the inspiration for this book.

In 1997, in Montclair, NJ, my wife's step father Ray passed away. My wife Donna was the executrix of his and her mother Blair's estate.

Ray was a CPA and during his marriage to Blair, he prepared a fabulous notebook with complete details about their life and desired future wishes. It contained everything those who followed him would need to manage their affairs: assets, financial records, important contacts, medical information and providers, final wishes, etc. This notebook was invaluable to Donna, especially during this time of sorrow, to perform her duties as executrix, as well as into the future to ensure that her mother was cared for as they both desired when Blair developed Alzheimers. That notebook was consulted many times when making decisions regarding Donna's mom.

In subsequent discussions with friends at our church in North Palm Beach, Florida, about situations where the first spouse died and the surviving spouse was left to "carry on", we frequently heard the cry for a "better way" to become prepared for that eventual day. These discussions led Donna and me to prepare and present, pro bono, seminars which we entitled "Suddenly Alone". All were enthusiastically received, which we appreciated. We were also encouraged to "publish" the notebook which was a by-product of these seminars.

This book is the result of that encouragement. We wish all of you the comfort that completing the templates in this book for your own notebook will provide; not only to you but also to your spouse and your heirs and their families. It truly is a gift from you to them.

Ken and Donna Wright

SUDDENLY ALONE© PERSONAL OPERATING MANUAL

Table of Contents

Section I PERSONAL, FINANCIAL, AND LEGAL DOCUMENTS 1

I: DEVELOPING A PERSONAL OPERATING MANUAL......................3

II: CONTACTS — Family, Friends, Professionals.........................6

III: PERSONAL IDENTIFICATION DOCUMENTS
      — Cards, Licenses, Passports 11

IV: GENERAL INFORMATION TEMPLATE: 12

V: PERSONAL INFORMATION — Birth, Marriage, Military, Education 13

VI: SPECIFIC LIST OF ASSETS:... 15

      a. Bank Assets—Checking, Savings, CDs
      b. Investments—Brokerage and Individually Held
         i. Stocks
         ii. Bonds
         iii. Mutual Funds
      c. Accounts Receivable
      d. Business Assets and Agreements
      e. Real Estate
      f. Titled Property
      g. Other

VII: TAX DEFERRED INCOME — IRAs................................16

VIII: OTHER INCOME — Annuities, Pensions, Profit Sharing, Social
      Security..17

IX: INSURANCE POLICIES...18

X: GENERAL 20

    1. FIVE IMPORTANT PARTS OF AN ESTATE PLAN................20

    2: OVERVIEW OF APPLICABLE DOCUMENTS 21

        a. LAST WILL AND TESTAMENT
        b. REVOC ABLE LIVING TRUST
        c. DURABLE POWER OF ATTORNEY FOR PROPERTY
        d. HEALTH CARE POWER OF ATTORNEY and HIPAA
           (Health Insurance Portability and Accountability Act of 1996)
           RELEASE AUTHORIZATION
        e. LIVING WILL and DO NOT RESUSCITATE (DNR)
           ORDER

    3. PROBATE...23

    4. ADDITIONAL ESTATE PLAN CONSIDERATIONS...............24

    5: LETTER OF INSTRUCTION 26

    6: YET ADDITIONAL ESTATE PLANNING INFORMATION
       — NEPTUNE SOCIETY 30

XI: MEDICAID CONSIDERATIONS......................................33

XII: Veterans long term care benefits..36

Section II SELF-CARE..37

XIII: A LIVING WISH...38

        a. BURIAL/CREMATION AND FUNERAL
           ARRANGEMENTS
        b. MEMORIAL
        c. OBITUARY

XIV: PERSONAL LIFE.. 44

        a. SAFETY Personal, Home, Vehicular 44
        b. BUDGET Income, Expenses, Online Tools 49
        c. MEDICAL Contacts, History, Prescriptions, Supplements,
           Tests 53

    d. APPOINTMENTS Medical, Recurring, Specific Events, Personal 54

    e. DAILY ACTIVITIES Devotional, Current Events, Calendar, Contacts, Mail, Filing, To Do List, Read File 56

XV: HOUSEHOLD 58

    a. HOUSEHOLD EQUIPMENT — Operation Manuals..........58

    b. HOUSEHOLD ITEMS THAT REQUIRE YOUR ATTENTION —Replacement, Repair, Cleaning, Inspection 58

    c. HOUSEHOLD SERVICE PROVIDERS AND FREQUENCY OF SERVICE 59

    d. HOUSEHOLD SECURITY: UTILITY CONNECTIONS AND KEYS— UTILITIES, SECURITY, EXTRA KEYS 59

    e. SAFE DEPOSIT BOX 61

    f. CONTENTS OF WALLET: CREDIT CARDS/MEDICAL CARDS/LICENSES 62

    g. COMPUTER NETWORK— Passwords, Software CDs, Manuals 63

XVI: LIVING INDEPENDENTLY 64

    a. Activity, Outdoors, Balance, Healthy Meals, Sleep, Stress Relief, Hydration, Personal Connections, Alcohol Moderation, Smoking Cessation, Positive Attitude, Sense of Humor, Support Group... 64

XVII: WHEN HELP IS NEEDED... 66

    a. COMMUNITY SUPPORT SERVICES — Meals, Transportation, Housekeeping, In-Home Care, Religious Affiliation, Elder Help Lines... 66

XVIII: WHEN IT IS TIME TO MOVE.......................................68

    a. GETTING RID OF "STUFF" — Inventory, List, Photo, Give Away, Sell...68

    b. SELLING YOUR HOUSE OR CONDO — Elder Specialists in Real Estate and Financial Services 69

    c. PREPARING TO MOVE — Floor Plan, Pack, Record Contents & Room 70

d. ALTERNATIVE LIVING ARRANGEMENTS — Rental or Purchase..70

    i. Independent
    ii. Assisted Living
    iii. Skilled Nursing
    iv. Memory Care
    v. Life Care Communities
    vi. Long Term Care Insurance

Section III TEMPLATES TO BE COMPLETED BY YOU............................75

Section IV CREDITS 123

SECTION I

PERSONAL, FINANCIAL, AND LEGAL DOCUMENTS

I: DEVELOPING A PERSONAL OPERATING MANUAL

1. A PLAN IS KEY:

It has often been said, that if you don't know where you are going, any road will take you there. To ensure a successful lifestyle, it helps to have a roadmap: A plan that articulates who and what you are and what you want done with your "stuff". At a minimum, it helps to record what "stuff" you have and where it is located.

There are many benefits to having your own written plan:

BENEFITS:

A written plan is informative and contains most of your important information in one place (your Suddenly Alone notebook). You, certainly, will realize a large amount of peace of mind, as will those close to you, your spouse, and your heirs. It prepares yourself and your family for the inevitable, and provides your spouse and heirs with a roadmap to all that is necessary for them to continue living effectively, without being "lost" in your absence. In addition, as we age, we need tools that supplement our abilities and enable us to lead a healthy lifestyle.

The Estate Planning section of your plan enables you to get your own financial affairs identified and in order. It establishes a complete reference and plan that is your specific choice for the ultimate distribution of your assets.

And, finally, it communicates your specific last wishes, eliminating any doubt by your loved ones as to what they might have been, at a time when doubt is least appreciated by them. You have provided the answers to their concerns in advance.

2. FORMAT:

a. THIS MANUAL CONTAINS TEMPLATES THAT WILL BECOME SPECIFIC TO YOU.

We have provided you with (many) pre-formatted templates which will enable you to be organized and clear.

b. THIS MANUAL UTILIZES THE "MAGIC OF A #2 PENCIL AND PIECES OF PAPER" (Portability and ease of completion).

Many years ago when I was attempting to convince the computer executives of my Wall Street customer of the benefits of a back-up data center, their Director of Engineering queried: "What good does all your additional computer stuff do if my staff develops Legionnaire's Disease?"! The value of a manual notebook would enable that employer to open for business in the morning, record its transactions and close at the end of the business day, preserving the important data for further processing once his organization was again fully functional.

Like that Director of Engineering, you will utilize paper and pencil to record, in one convenient and portable notebook, everything that is essential to administer your affairs, via the templates we have developed for that purpose. It is our intent to provide, in the near future, an electronic set of templates that can be completed and maintained online by you and from which multiple copies might be made for your relatives and friends. For now, however, paper and pencil are the tools we will use!

To get one free set of templates which you can print out and copy, email us at suddenlyalone3@gmail.com. Limit one set per book owner. Yes, there are many templates to be completed. Maybe, not all of them will pertain to you. Simply utilize those that do and ignore the rest. The secret is to take your time, working with one template at a time, as there are often decisions and data gathering required on your part to successfully complete each template.

The "good news" is that we have designed these templates with a "learning curve of 1" (easy to use the first time your try!).

In the design of my employer's first automatic teller machines (ATM's) our product design engineers had a special Human Factors laboratory to ensure that our ATM's could be successfully used by anyone the first time they tried. Your authors are now "senior citizens" and appreciate "simple" and "easy to use". We have designed these templates to be easy to use by you.

We have collected full size templates together in the last section of this book. You can utilize these full size templates to make additional copies for your family and heirs. Be sure to keep one set of "blank" templates to use as "a Master set", should you want to revise templates after initially completing them. To get a free complete set of templates which you can print out and copy, email us at suddenlyalone3@gmail.com. Limit one set per book owner.

3. **THE PROCESS:**

    Complete each template with the information requested. Pay attention to instructions particular to each template.

    Keep copies (not the originals) of specific documents in this book, along with their relevant templates. Be sure to record the safe location of each original document noted on each template (We use 3-hole sheet protectors to hold these copies in our notebook).

    Complete only those templates that relate to you. Not everyone will need all the templates that are included in this book.

II: CONTACTS

This template section collects and records contact information for family, friends, professionals, etc.

Be sure to make multiple copies of the "Relatives and Close Friends" template as the one page included in this book will not be sufficient to record all of these people.

Again, fill in only those specific contacts that you actually have. Leave the rest blank. We have included a sample "Attorney" contact which is actually the real attorney we used for our Living Trust. We strongly suggest you avail yourselves of a certified "Elder Law" attorney in your home state to draft a living trust for you and your family. You will see the benefits of such a trust in subsection "Overview of Estate Documents", subsection "Probate" and in subsection "Additional Estate Plan Considerations". The templates that follow this page are also included in SECTION III: TEMPLATES TO BE COMPLETED BY YOU. To get one free set of templates from Section III, which you can print and copy email us at suddenlyalone3@gmail.com. Limit one set per book owner.

KEY ADVISORS TO BE CONTACTED:

ACCOUNTANT: _____

Phone: _____ Firm: _____

Address: _____

ATTORNEY: <u>THE KARP LAW FIRM, P.A.</u> _____

Phone: <u>(561) 625-1100</u> _____

Address: _____

AUTO INSURANCE AGENT: _____

Phone: _____ Firm: _____

Address: _____

BANK: _____

Phone: _____ Firm: _____

Address: _____

CLERGY: _____

Phone: _____ Church/Synagogue: _____

Address: _____

DOCTOR: _____

Phone: _____ **Hospital:** _____

Address: _____

EMPLOYER: _____

Phone: _____ **Firm:** _____

Address: _____

FINANCIAL ADVISOR: _____

Phone: _____ **Firm:** _____

Address: _____

FUNERAL DIRECTOR: _____

Phone: _____ **Firm:** _____

Address: _____

GENERAL INSURANCE AGENT: _____

Phone: _____ **Firm:** _____

Address: _____

LANDLORD: _____

Phone: _____ **Firm** _____

Address _____

LIFE INSURANCE AGENT: _____

Phone: _____ **Firm** _____

Address _____

PARTNER: _____

Phone: _____ **Firm** _____

Address _____

STOCKBROKER: _____

Phone: _____ **Firm** _____

Address _____

TRUST OFFICER: _____

Phone: _____ **Institution** _____

Address _____

RELATIVES AND CLOSE FRIENDS TO BE CONTACTED (BE SURE TO MAKE MULTIPLE COPIES OF THIS SPECIFIC TEMPLATE TO CONTAIN ALL OF YOUR RELATIVES AND FRIENDS)

NAME _____

Relationship _____ **Phone** _____

Address _____

NAME _____

Relationship _____ **Phone** _____

Address _____

NAME _____

Relationship _____ **Phone** _____

Address _____

NAME _____

Relationship _____ **Phone** _____

Address _____

NAME _____

Relationship _____ **Phone** _____

Address _____

III: PERSONAL IDENTIFICATION DOCUMENTS

(List each item and where the original is located and make a copy of each to be inserted here).

This is the section where you record your personal identification documents information including a copy of each document to be included (several should fit on one copy page). Be sure to note here where the original of each of these documents is located. Make as many separate copy pages as you need to collect all of your Personal Identification documents.

Below is a sample listing of personal identification documents:

DOCUMENTS: WHERE LOCATED:

- **LICENSES**
  - o **DRIVERS**
  - o **PROFESSIONAL**
  - o **FISHING/HUNTING**
- **PASSPORTS**
- **PERMITS**
  - o **CONCEALED WEAPONS**
- **MEMBERSHIPS/ASSOCIATIONS**
  - o **CLUBS**
  - o **AAA**
  - o **AARP**

IV: GENERAL INFORMATION TEMPLATE:

Much of your important information would fit into this "General Information" category. Those listed below are just a sample of what you may have.

Subsection V: "Personal Information" also contains important Personal legal documents such as Birth Certificates, Marriage License, Military Records, Social Security Cards, etc.

The primary purpose of both of these templates is to contain in one place the locations of your important documents.

MISCELLANEOUS:

My safe deposit box is located at: _____

The keys to the safe deposit box are located at: _____

My personal safe is located at: _____

My tax records are located at: _____

Other: _____

V: PERSONAL INFORMATION

(Keep copies of the following documents in this book): _____

Birth certificate: Original located at: _____

Marriage license: Original located at: _____

Military Records: Original located at: _____

Social Security Card: Original located at: _____

Judgments from any court cases affecting me (e.g. divorce, etc.) are located at:

_____

Miscellaneous papers of personal interest are located at: _____

INDICATE WHERE THE ORIGINAL ITEMS LISTED OR COPIED BELOW ARE LOCATED:

Past Income Tax Returns: _____

Divorce/Separation papers: _____

Adoption papers: _____

Death Certificates: _____

Citizenship papers: _____

Passports: _____

Leases/Mortgages: _____

Instructions Upon Death _____

Family Albums: _____

Autobiography or family tree/history: _____

Favorite photos: _____

VI: SPECIFIC LIST OF ASSETS:

We have included 10 different Asset List templates (#1- 10) to record all of your non tax-deferred (IRA) assets: Bank Accounts, Investment Accounts, Accounts Receivable, Business Assets and Agreements, Real Estate, Titled property, and "Other" (a "catch-all" template for assets we may have overlooked).

Three Tax deferred assets templates are described in a separate subsection.

Again, the purpose of these templates is to record, in one place, each of the above assets so that your family and heirs will not have to tear your house apart trying to identify what assets you own when you are no longer able to tell them (due to incapacity or death) what assets you own and where they are.

We have separate templates for investment assets held directly by you versus investment assets held by your broker. Be sure to read the Asset templates heading very carefully to understand which type of asset that specific template is for.

VII: TAX DEFERRED INCOME

Three Tax deferred income templates (# 11-13) include IRA's, Tax deferred Annuities, Pensions, Profit Sharing, and Other future income sources. You will want to record the identity of each of these items, the company that sourced them (if any) and the name(s) of any beneficiaries and/or contingencies associated with these items.

VIII: OTHER INCOME

Other income includes Social Security, Interest bearing accounts, Dividends, etc.

IX: INSURANCE

This section includes two Insurance templates (# 15-16) for Life Insurance, Non Tax-Deferred Annuities, and Other types of insurance: Disability, Medical, Auto, Homeowners, Windstorm, Umbrella, Flood, Other Liability, and Other.

<u>X-XII: ESTATE PLANNING CONSIDERATIONS</u>

X: GENERAL
XI: MEDICAID
XII: VETERANS BENEFITS

X: GENERAL

1. FIVE IMPORTANT PARTS OF AN ESTATE PLAN

A. **LAST WILL AND TESTAMENT:** Allows you to decide who receives your personal and real property; who will be the guardian of your minor children; who will manage and distribute your estate as your executor/ executrix; provides for setting up trusts for minors or incapacitated persons that will be beneficiaries; and things of that nature upon your death. If you die intestate (without a will) your estate will be subject to state law and can be more costly and difficult to probate.

B. **REVOCABLE LIVING TRUST:** A living trust takes effect while you are still alive and allows you to make sure your assets are protected and managed according to your specific wishes. If revocable, it gives you the flexibility of changing or dissolving the trust at any time. If irrevocable it cannot be changed or terminated regardless of circumstances. Living trusts are private and allow your survivors to avoid probate; therefore, assets immediately go to the beneficiary(s). Unfortunately, they do not allow you to name a personal guardian for your minor children, may not save on taxes, and could allow creditors to tap into the assets of the trust.

C. **DURABLE POWER OF ATTORNEY (DPOA):** An executed Durable Power of Attorney allows you to appoint someone to make financial and other decisions (generally not medical ones which require a HIPAA DPOA) ON YOUR BEHALF. This appointment can take effect immediately or can be delayed until the event of your incapacity and inability to make decisions on your own.

D. **MEDICAL (HEALTH CARE) POWER OF ATTORNEY OR DESIGNATION OF HEALTH CARE AGENT (ALSO HIPAA RELEASE AND POWER OF ATTORNEY):** Enables you to appoint a representative to assume responsibility for health related decisions in the event of your future incapacity (grant or withhold medical treatment, employ doctors, nurses, etc., arrange for hospital or nursing home care, provide for organ donation, according to your wishes). HIPPA RELEASE AND

POWER OF ATTORNEY ARE OFTEN INCLUDED WITHIN THIS PART.

E. **LIVING WILL AND DO NOT RESUSCITATE (DNR):** A competent individual (You) may execute a document directing whether or not you want the use of life-sustaining procedures in the event you have an incurable or irreversible terminal condition.

NOTE: All of these documents may vary from state to state, but are generally of this nature. Your estate plan includes important documents that should be kept in a safe place. Access to your safe deposit box may be temporarily impeded so you may wish to give copies to your executor and/or other family members. At a minimum, keep a copy in your notebook and tell someone where it is located.

2: OVERVIEW OF APPLICABLE DOCUMENTS

The preceding pages on Estate Planning contain several references to important documents (DPOA, REVOCABLE LIVING TRUST, HEALTHCARE POA, HIPAA RELEASE POA, LIVING WILL AND DNR).

In order to clarify which documents are to be used when, we have prepared the following table that identifies which of these documents are needed based on a specific life event: Period of Incapacity, Terminal Condition, or Death. Some of these documents are needed in more than one of these life events and are so noted.

The following table illustrates these life events and the appropriate documents that would pertain to these events. Note that some of the important documents identified are used in more than one life event (DPOA, Revocable Living Trust)

LIFE EVENT	DOCUMENT	PURPOSE
PERIOD OF INCAPACITY	**DURABLE POWER OF ATTORNEY (DPOA)**	A DPOA gives someone you designate the power to make financial decisions on your behalf.
	REVOCABLE LIVING TRUST	A REVOCABLE LIVING TRUST allows your successor trustee to manage trust assets for you in the event of incapacity.

	HEALTH CARE POWER OF ATTORNEY	A HEALTHCARE POWER OF ATTORNEY gives someone you designate the power to make health care decisions for you
	HIPAA RELEASE (Health Industry Portability Accountability Act 1996)	A HIPAA RELEASE allows your medical provider to share your medical information with the designated person(s) making decisions on your behalf
TERMINAL PERIOD	DPOA LIVING WILL	A LIVING WILL gives you the option to choose which life-sustaining measures are or are not acceptable to you
	DNR (Do Not Resuscitate)	DNR gives you the option not to be resuscitated in the event you are incapacitated.*
		*FLORIDA NOTE: Must be an original (on yellow paper), signed by a doctor. Also only works in hospital recovery room (not in Surgi-centers, emergency rooms, first responders, etc.)
UPON DEATH	LAST WILL AND TESTAMENT	LAST WILL AND TESTAMENT designates the executor of your estate, the guardian of your minor children, if applicable, and how your estate is to be distributed.
	REVOCABLE LIVING TRUST	A REVOCABLE LIVING TRUST, in addition to characteristics of a will, may avoid probate, preserve privacy and provide protection in the case of incapacity
	LETTER OF INSTRUCTION	A LETTER OF INSTRUCTION allows you to detail which specific items of tangible personal property are going to whom (a level of detail not always covered in a will).

IMPORTANT ESTATE DOCUMENTS LISTING:

"I have these documents dated _____

Located _____

Executor: _____

Prepared by: _____

3. PROBATE

Probate is the process whereby a state court publicly confirms the will's validity and/or establishes which parties inherit the estate, inventories, and assets; pays debts and distributes property. Probate is time consuming for the people you leave behind, but provides court protection for heirs and beneficiaries. It also cuts off the claims of creditors after a period of time following the issuance of Letters Testamentary (Usually a brief, one page document issued by the county clerk which simply states that the person identified in the letter is currently serving in the capacity of **independent executor** or **independent executrix** of an estate which is being probated)

LIVING TRUST

A living trust takes effect while you are still alive and allows you to make sure your assets are protected and managed according to your specific wishes. If revocable, it gives you the flexibility of changing or dissolving the trust at any time. If irrevocable it cannot be changed or terminated regardless of circumstances. Living trusts are private and allow your survivors to avoid probate; therefore, assets immediately go to the beneficiary(s). Unfortunately, they do not allow you to name a personal guardian for your minor children, may not save on taxes, and could allow creditors to tap into the assets of the trust.

Also, living trusts will not transfer assets automatically that were not specifically mentioned. If you create a living trust, make sure to include a "POUR OVER WILL" clause in your will that bequeaths assets to your living trust.

QUALIFIED INCOME TRUST:

A trust can be established which enables otherwise income ineligible Medicaid applicants to qualify for Medicaid. It is called a Qualified Income Trust (or Miller Trust). This can be beneficial when you may receive excess income and cannot qualify for Medicaid, but that excess amount is not enough income to pay for the average cost of a nursing home. Since every state may not have this type of trust, it is necessary to seek proper counsel.

4. ADDITIONAL ESTATE PLAN CONSIDERATIONS

A. **INCLUDE A HERITAGE TRUST WITHIN YOUR LIVING TRUST TO INSURE YOUR ASSETS STAY WITH YOUR CHILDREN AND NOT IN-LAW RELATIONS.** This addition to your Living Trust will ensure that whatever assets you leave to your children will remain and be restricted to "blood relatives" only. This is helpful if in the future one of your children unfortunately pre-decease his/her spouse who thereafter marries someone of less than desirable repute who might otherwise put your heir's inheritance at risk.

B. **HAVE YOUR BANK(S) REVIEW YOUR DURABLE POWER OF ATTORNEY (DPOA) BEFORE IT NEEDS TO BE USED:**
   a. Banks can refuse to honor DPOA when presented.
   b. Have banks accept DPOA or indicate what is needed for DPOA to be accepted.
   c. Get a receipt.
   d. Get bank approval in writing.
   e. Furnish your DPOA agent with a copy of the approval letter.

C. **CHANGE (OR MAKE) YOUR EXISTING REVOCABLE TRUST TO INCLUDE A "CO-TRUSTEE" IN ADDITION TO A "SUCCESSOR TRUSTEE(S)":**
   a. Advantage: a co-trustee can avoid bureaucratic hassles more easily than a successor trustee can.
   b. Co-trustees do not need to furnish medical documentation of your incapacity in order to access items in your trust.
   c. Important to advise your financial institutions that you have done so and put the co-trustee on the signature card.

D. **WHERE IS YOUR *ORIGINAL* WILL?**
   a. Probate courts will only accept your original will.
   b. A copy is not acceptable. The legal presumption is that *you intended to destroy the original will* if a copy is presented.
   c. Without the original will, your probatable assets will pass under your state's intestacy law, requiring your heir's time consuming

and expensive legal action to establish that the deceased *did not intend to destroy the orignal will.*

    d. Keep track of your original will, its location, and make sure someone you know and trust knows where it is.

E. BECOME FAMILIAR WITH YOUR STATE'S "MEDICAID MANAGED CARE PROGRAM" IF ONE EXISTS.

F. SMART "SMART PHONE" USAGE: FOR QUICK HEALTH CARE DECISIONS, HAVE YOUR HEALTH CARE POWER OF ATTORNEY AND LIVING WILL SCANNED TO YOUR SMART PHONE AND/OR EMAILED TO YOUR AGENT'S SMART PHONE SO THEY ARE AVAILABLE BY YOUR AGENT AT ANY TIME AND FROM ANY LOCATION. It is very probable that your DPOA agent will not likely be near the filing cabinet where you keep your DPOA and Living Will when you need him/her to produce it but rather pretty close to wherever you might be at the moment of need (hospital, clinic, etc.) Your agent's smart phone will be able to produce your DPOA and Living Will immediately if it is on his/her smart phone.

G. OPTIMIZE YOUR CHILDREN'S USE OF INHERITING YOUR IRA/401 K'S (SINCE THEY ARE YOUNGER THAN YOU):
    a. Establish an "IRA STRETCHOUT TRUST":
    Your child's life expectancy replaces yours as the basis for starting required minimum distributions (RMD). This also restricts your child's withdrawals to his/her RMD amounts enabling the IRA to last for your child's life expectancy (rather than your beneficiary withdrawing all at once and possibly squandering the assets).
    b. INCLUDE A "POUR-OVER WILL" CLAUSE IN YOUR WILL TO INCLUDE ANY ASSETS YOU MIGHT ACQUIRE AFTER THE DATE OF YOUR WILL. Any assets you own and identify in your will should be distributed per your letter of instruction within your will. Any assets you may acquire after the date of your will are not covered by your letter of instruction and, in fact, are subject to probate UNLESS: you include a "Pour-Over" Clause in your will that simply states "that your will and letter of

instruction are to include any and all assets that you may acquire after the date of your will and own at the time of your death".

5: LETTER OF INSTRUCTION

Your Estate Planning Letter and Letters of Instruction are very critical to making sure that your wishes for actions after your death and equally for the distribution of your assets will be done according to your specific wishes. This particular document has meant the difference between a deceased's wishes being carried out in spite of legal challenges to the will and representations of the deceased by direct and indirect family members. Sadly, we are seeing increased incidents of legal actions by heirs which necessitates this document. Letters of Instruction provide a mechanism whereby you can update an already existing Estate Plan as you acquire additional assets and/or change your wishes about end of life arrangements. You should send your updated Letters of Instruction to the attorney who prepared your Estate documents. Specifically:

The Letter of Instruction "Distribution of Personal Property – Exhibit A" specifies how you want your personal property to be distributed The Letter of Instruction "Funeral Instructions – Exhibit B" states your personal wishes about last rites and burial services, if any. In the SELF CARE section a "LIVING WISH" form is provided which offers you an opportunity to state your specific instructions for the care of your body and the events following your death.

Also, often, your surviving family members might have ideas of how to handle your funeral, burial, etc. that are at odds with your wishes. Again, this Letter of Instruction goes a long way to leaving no doubt as to what YOUR last wishes are, and were. While it will not legally prevent your heirs from acting contrary to your last wishes, it does make it difficult for them to contend that your last wishes were not known.

Again: Write your own obituary. Now. Who knows you better than you?!

ESTATE PLANNING LETTER

OF

(YOUR NAME GOES HERE)

_____

DISTRIBUTION OF PERSONAL PROPERTY:

I HAVE ATTACHED AS "EXHIBIT A" TO THIS LETTER MY PERSONAL WISHES CONCERNING DISTRIBUTION OF MY PERSONAL EFFECTS.

FUNERAL INSTRUCTIONS:

I HAVE ATTACHED AS "EXHIBIT B" TO THIS LETTER MY PERSONAL WISHES CONCERNING LAST RITES AND BURIAL SERVICES.

(EXHIBITS "A" AND "B" FOLLOW THIS PAGE)

OTHER DIRECTIONS TO MY FAMILY:

_____
_____
_____
_____
_____
_____
_____
_____
_____
_____

ESTATE PLANNING LETTER

OF

(YOUR NAME GOES HERE)

EXHIBIT "A"

DISTRIBUTION OF PERSONAL PROPERTY

DESCRIPTION OF PROPERTY: BENEFICIARY:

1._____

2._____

3._____

4._____

5._____

6._____

7._____

8._____

9._____

10._____

11._____

SIGNATURE: _____

ESTATE PLANNING LETTER

OF

(YOUR NAME GOES HERE)

_____

EXHIBIT "B"

BURIAL AND FUNERAL INSTRUCTIONS

DIRECTIONS FOR MEMORIAL SERVICE:_____
_____
_____
_____

BURIAL:

    MY BODY SHOULD BE BURIED IN_____**CEMETERY**

    LOCATED IN_____

    MY BODY SHOULD BE CREMATED AND THE ASHES
_____
_____

    MY BODY SHOULD BE DONATED TO: _____

    OTHER, SPECIFY _____

SPECIFIC COMMENTS, WISHES, THOUGHTS, ETC.: _____
_____

SIGNATURE: _____**DATE:**_____

6: YET ADDITIONAL ESTATE PLANNING INFORMATION

FROM THE NEPTUNE SOCIETY: CREMATION PLANNING & INFORMATION BOOKLET:

At the risk of being repetitive, we are including the following information from the Neptune Society which does an excellent job of articulating important estate planning information:

Check List for Family/Executor:

Following the cremation and interment of a loved one, the reality of the business of death begins. The following checklist will assist your family and executor and help determine how many certified copies of the death certificate are needed.

- Locate the deceased's will and deliver it to a probate attorney for filing with the proper court.

- Deliver to the attorney a list of assets to be in included in the probate estate and liabilities.

- Keep accurate records of all receipts to and disbursements from the probate estate. Establish an estate checking account to deposit probate assets and pay final bills, such as medical bills.

- Do not distribute any probate assets without court approval.

- Change over bank accounts where the deceased had a loan. They will inform you if the loan was covered by credit life insurance and what needs to be done to file the appropriate claim.

- Gather all the bills, even credit cards, to make you aware of all the credit obligations of the deceased. Many installment loans and service contracts can be covered by credit life insurance, which pays off the account balance upon the death of the customer.

- Contact sources of retirement funds and pension plans that the deceased was receiving and apply for benefits that are due.

- Change utilities records and remove the deceased's name. Change the phone book listing to show your first initial and last name to avert prank calls.

- Settle life insurance claims and contact health insurance companies to stop coverage on the deceased. Revise your own insurance needs.

- Income tax return(s) will have to be filed for the year of death.

- Change the deed on property, which is usually done in the county where the property is located, unless it is already in a living trust.

- Change the title and registration on vehicles with the Department of Motor Vehicles, unless they are in the name of a living trust.

- Contact Social Security and the Veteran's Administration to file for any benefits.

PLAN YOUR ESTATE

As important as advance planning for your burial or cremation is, so is planning your estate. If you have not already done so, now is the time to plan your estate so you can protect yourself and the ones you love for the future and ensure your wishes will be carried through.

Knowing that your estate is in order can give you peace of mind and it will ensure that the futures of the ones you love will be protected. Don't let the state decide who receives your assets. Make sure your wishes concerning your medical care will be honored when you can no longer speak for yourself.

DISCUSS MATTERS WITH YOUR FAMILY

Gathering your family and loved one's to discuss your death is not easy to do, but it is an essential part of planning your estate. Meeting with your family and discussing your wishes might possibly prevent problems in the future. You might choose to disclose a few specifics. This may help your family understand why you have made the decisions you have and in turn, you would hope they will honor your wishes. Or, you may not want to give any specific details at all of what you intend to do. Often times, discussing your plans in general terms and expressing the thought you have put into them can be sufficient.

WHEN TO UPDATE YOUR ESTATE PLAN

Planning your estate is an on-going process. If you marry, divorce, move to another state, have a child, if a spouse or child dies, or you experience a significant change in your financial condition, you should update your estate plan so it accurately represents your current wishes.

You must never try to change your documents yourself by making cross outs, erasures, or interlineations. This is not a legal way to make changes and a court may later find it invalid or ignore the changes. Be sure to consult appropriate legal counsel to do these updates.

If you do not comply with the law when signing your estate planning documents, they may later be deemed to be invalid. Be sure to comply with all the formal execution requirements in your state when signing your estate planning documents so that they are not invalid, incomplete or able to be altered by someone else. Again, engage legal counsel to perform any changes required.

IMPORTANT QUESTIONS TO ASK YOURSELF

As you begin to think about your estate plan, consider the following questions:

1. Who do I want to inherit my property?
2. What assets will I be leaving behind?
3. Are my assets owned jointly or separately?
4. Do I have assets over a certain value that will subject my heirs or my estate to estate tax?
5. If my spouse remarries after I die, does this change my mind about what to do with my property?
6. What if my spouse or other beneficiaries die before I do?
7. Are my heirs old enough to handle their inheritance?
8. Would I like to leave donations to any charitable organizations or institutions?
9. Who do I want to be the executor of my estate?
10. Who will I choose to be the guardian of my minor children?
11. Who will make my health care decisions if I can't (HIPAA DPOA DNR)?
12. Under what circumstances would I want my life support discontinued?

END OF NEPTUNE SOCIETY ESTATE PLANNING INFORMATION

XI: MEDICAID CONSIDERATIONS

Estate planning
Medicaid considerations

1. Income requirements:
   o Self: monthly income cannot exceed $2,199 (1/1/15).
   o Community (spouse) income: no limit on spouse monthly income.
2. Asset requirements:
   o If not in a nursing home:
     ▪ Self: may not own countable assets over $2,000
     ▪ Community spouse: may retain up to $119,220 (7/1/15)
   o If both spouses are in a nursing home:
     ▪ Together may retain maximum of $3,000 countable assets plus any exempt and non-available assets.
   o Asset definitions:
     ▪ Available (countable).
       • Assets available to the applicant and/or spouse.
     ▪ Non-available.
       • Assets not counted by Medicaid to determine eligibility: applicant or spouse has no means of accessing them or readily liquidating them (rental real estate).
     ▪ Exempt.
       • Assets not counted by Medicaid to determine eligibility:
         o Homestead if equity is $552,000 or less (1/1/15).
         o Motor vehicle: 1 motor vehicle is exempt regardless of age; a 2nd vehicle if it is over 7 years old and not a luxury, antique, or customized vehicle.
         o Personal property: all except certain valuable art or jewelry.
         o Life insurance:

- Applicant: exempt if face value does not exceed $2,500 (1/1/15). Term policies are exempt. Cash value of policy is included in the $2,500 asset value of applicant.

- Spouse: exempt if face value does not exceed $2,500 (1/1/15). Term policies exempt.

o Burial plans:

- Applicant: up to $2,500 or unlimited if an irrevocable prepaid plan.

- Spouse: same as applicant.

o IRA's, 401k's, 403b's: qualified plans are considered "hybrids" by Florida Medicaid (assets or income): if applicant or spouse is already drawing from the plan monthly on an actuarially sound basis it is treated as income. If the plan is not being drawn down, it is treated as an asset.

o (Be sure to research what your particular state's rules are regarding these Medicaid exclusions).

3. Look back periods:

o Transfers by applicant or spouse before 1/1/10: 3 years if not made to/from a trust; 5 years if to/from a trust.

o Transfers by applicant or spouse after 1/1/10: all transfers have a 5 year look back period.

4. Adanced Medicaid planning techniques (if no long term care insurance):

o Irrevocable income-only trust:

- Objective here is to trigger the start of your look back period in advance of the time when the trust creator actually needs the benefits.

- Spouse may not be a trustee.

- You retain the right to remove/replace a trustee if not performing to your satisfaction

- You are not in "control" of your assets (your trustee is) but you are "in charge" (direct trustee to do what you want done with your assets).

o Medicaid gifting trust:

  ■ Gifting during a look back period can be problematical.

  ■ Medicaid gifting trust circumvents this problem.

  ■ Irrevocable: spouse may not serve as a trustee.

  ■ Establishing a Medicaid gifting trust triggers the 5 year look back period.

  ■ Once the 5 years have passed, any funds gifted from it or remaining in it are Medicaid exempt.

From: Guide to Medicaid Benefits for Long-term Nursing Care Costs by Joseph S. Karp

XII: VETERANS LONG TERM CARE BENEFITS

1. Web site for information: www.veteransaid.org.
2. Aid and attendance pension:
    a. Established 1952.
    b. For veterans and their surviving spouses.
    c. Provides attendance of a daily living care giver (eating, bathing, dressing, medication monitoring, etc.).
    d. Application process is complicated.
    e. To qualify:
        i. Honorable discharge with at least 90 days active duty service and at least 1 day served during a war-time period.
        ii. Medical diagnosis requiring daily assistance with 2 or more daily living activities.
        iii. Insufficient monthly income to purchase required care.
        iv. Limited liquid assets.
    f. Contact Veterans Affairs: 1-800-827-1000.
3. Improved pension benefits:
    a. Does not require veteran to have sustained a disability during military service.
    b. V.A. pension is considered "non-service connected compensation".
    c. Veteran or widow(er) qualification requirements:
        i. Veteran served at least 90 days active duty with at least 1 day during a war-time period (other than active duty for training).
        ii. Discharge must be other than dishonorable.
        iii. Veteran must have limited income and assets available.
        iv. Claimant must be 65 or older or have a permanent and total disability that occurred without the willful misconduct of the claimant.
        v. Veteran or widow(er) must sign an application and provide the application to the Veterans Administration.

From: Guide to Veterans Benefits for Long-term Care Expenses by Joseph S. Karp

SECTION II

SELF-CARE

Whether we are living alone or with someone else, it is important that we practice self-care. This section is all about ourselves: what we want to be done with our body after we die and what we can do to take care of ourselves to live a long and healthy life until we pass on.

XIII: A LIVING WISH, Template 17

The pastor at our church in Upper Montclair, New Jersey encouraged our congregation to use *A Living Wish* form to document instructions for the events following our physical death. We have modified this form to include additional information and will describe its contents. See A LIVING WISH, Template 17.

INSTRUCTIONS FOLLOWING MY PHYSICAL DEATH

A. Immediately following your death the funeral director and clergy should be notified at once.

B. Funeral Director. Now is the time to select your funeral director. You can call friends for the name of a funeral director they have used successfully or use the Yellow Pages or Internet to find a funeral director in your community. Schedule a visit to determine if the funeral home will be able to accommodate your wishes and is a place where your family and friends will feel comfortable after you are gone. Decide if you want to be placed in a coffin and if so, whether the coffin will be open or closed during visitation and/or the service. The price of a coffin varies greatly. It is wise to designate the type of coffin you would like, so that your family does not have to make that decision after you pass on. If you choose to be cremated, your body can be placed in a coffin or a cardboard box before the cremation process. You should specify in what type of container you would like your ashes placed. The container can range from a cardboard box to an elaborate urn. Write in the name and telephone number of the funeral director that you have selected.

C. Clergy. Attend a funeral or memorial service conducted by your minister, priest or rabbi to get ideas on how you would like your service to be performed. Write in the name and telephone number of the individual you want to officiate at your service.

D. Think about how you would like to have your body handled and describe your wishes in THE CARE OF MY BODY section of the form.

E. Document the components you would like to have included in your funeral or memorial service in THE SERVICE section of the form.

F. List the names and telephone numbers of the people who should be notified of your death: the lawyer who has copies of your will and other legal documents; family members; and close friends. Attach additional pages if needed.

THE CARE OF MY BODY

A. Based on your religious and personal preferences you should make a decision now as to whether you want your body buried or cremated. Burial is often chosen because a family plot already exists or burial is a family or religious tradition. Being able to visit a cemetery where a loved one is buried, often provides comfort to family members. However the cost of acquiring and maintaining a cemetery plot is a factor to be considered. You should select a cemetery now and consider acquiring a plot for yourself and your loved ones who would like to be buried there as well. Check with the cemetery about the number of caskets or cremation boxes that can be placed in one plot. Discuss with the cemetery personnel the options for interment before or following the service and document your preference. Indicate where you keep the deed for the cemetery plot so your loved ones can locate it.

Cremation is a process where the body is placed in a fiberboard box in open flames of 1600 – 2000 degrees Fahrenheit for one to three hours. The remains are cooled on a tray and weigh about four to eight pounds. If cremation is selected you can make prepaid arrangements now. A sample pre-need cremation offering will be discussed later. If you prefer to be cremated, you should specify where you would like your remains to be placed. The remains can be divided if you would like some of your ashes to be buried and others to be scattered such as in a garden or at sea. The mother of a friend of ours asked her daughter to scatter her remains at various places around the world and left money for her daughter to make the trip to do so.

B. Consider if you would like to donate parts of your body to a medical facility for transplant or research. Make arrangements with the appropriate medical authority for donation of your eyes, skin, organs, or body. Indicate where the papers that document your permission are kept.

C. There are different levels of embalming with associated costs. It is helpful to let your loved ones know your preference here.

D. If you want a specific type of coffin make your desires known so you can protect your family from making a costly choice that is not your wish. If you want your remains placed in a cemetery vault it is wise to discuss the options for the type of vault with the cemetery personnel so that your family will know your choice in advance.

THE SERVICE

A. Specify where you would like to have your funeral or memorial service held: in a house of worship or at the funeral home. You might also consider a graveside service or other location.

B. Think about what spiritual readings you would like to have at your service, whom you would like to read these passages at your service, and make a note of them.

C. Write down the musical selections you would like at your service.

D. Record other thoughts about your service such as the names of people that you would like to speak on your behalf.

E. If you want your body present at the service in either an open or closed casket indicate your preference. If your body has been cremated, you might want to suggest a photo or picture of yourself be present at the service.

F. If you have favorite flowers, suggest that your loved ones have them at your service. Some people prefer to invite friends to make a donation to a favorite charity in lieu of sending flowers to the family.

A MEMORIAL

If you would like a memorial upon your death, indicate your wishes here. Some houses of worship and/or communities have memorial gardens, memorial plaques, memorial bricks, etc. where you might like to be acknowledged.

Some of our friends have had a laminated card prepared by the family or funeral home that includes the dates of birth and death of the deceased, a picture of the deceased, and a Bible verse, prayer, or favorite saying.

PRE-NEED CREMATION ARRANGEMENTS

Since we have chosen to be cremated after our death, we made pre-need cremation arrangements. There are many organizations and funeral homes that will help you to plan your arrangements and enable you to pay for them now. We selected the Neptune Society at www.neptunesociety.com. When one of us dies, a family member or friend can call the Neptune Society's toll free number. The Neptune Society picks up and transports the body to a holding facility; collects the information needed for the death certificate and procures the doctor's signature; obtains authorization from the medical examiner to cremate the body; performs the cremation; and ships the remains to the location specified by the family. We paid an additional fee for transportation of the body from anywhere in the world to the cremation site. The Neptune Society also provides a memento package that includes a very informative "Cremation Planning & Information Book." We have included examples of pages from this book.

If you have made pre-need cremation arrangements, indicate this in "OTHER WISHES" at the end of A LIVING WISH, Template 17, and include the name, address, and telephone number of the provider of these services for your family's use.

BENEFITS FOR VETERANS AND DEPENDENTS

If you are a Veteran, there are additional options for your burial and benefits that are available for your dependents. It is recommended that you contact the Department of Veteran's Affairs and speak with a Veteran's Benefit Counselor at 800-827-1000 or go online at www.cem.va.gov to determine your eligibility. Proof of your military service is substantiated by your military discharge paper, Report of Separation, DD Form 214. If you are not able to locate your military records, you can request them by completing standard form SF-180 which can be obtained online at www.archives.gov/veterans or by mail from the National Personnel Records Center, attn: Military Personnel Records, One Archives Drive, St. Louis MO 63138.

Since your Report of Separation, DD Form 214 is needed by your next of kin to obtain Veteran's benefits on your behalf, be sure that you have your Report of

Separation, DD Form 214 in your Suddenly Alone Notebook. You may want to investigate your eligibility and your desire for the following Veteran's benefits: burial expenses and funeral costs, a burial flag, a Presidential Memorial Certificate, burial in a National Cemetery, headstones and markers, and survivor benefits. Indicate the Veteran's benefits you want and are eligible for in "OTHER WISHES" at the end of A LIVING WISH, Template 17, so that your survivors will know which benefits to apply for in recognition of your service.

Contact information for veterans and dependents is noted below:

BENEFITS FOR VETERANS AND DEPENDENTS.

>**DEPARTMENT OF VETERANS AFFAIRS**
>>800-827-1000 OR <u>WWW.VA.GOV</u>.

>**REIMBURSEMENT OF BURIAL EXPENSES AND FUNERAL COSTS.**
>**VA FORM 21-530 APPLICATION FOR BURIAL ALLOWANCE**
>>800-827-1000 OR <u>WWW.CEM.VA.GOV</u>.

>**BURIAL FLAGS.**
>**VA FORM 21-2008, APPLICATION FOR US FLAG FOR BURIAL.**

>**PRESIDENTIAL MEMORIAL CERTIFICATES.**
>**VA FORM 40-0247 PRESIDENTIAL MEMORIAL CERTIFICATE REQUEST**
>>800-827-1000.

>**BURIAL IN NATIONAL CEMETERIES.**
>**ARLINGTON NATIONAL CEMETERY**
>>703-607-8000 OR <u>WWW.ARLINGTONCEMETERY.MIL</u>.

>**STATE VETERAN CEMETERY**
>**WWW.CEM.VA.GOV**

>**HEADSTONES AND MARKERS.**
>>800- 697-6947.

SURVIVOR BENEFITS.
WWW.VA.GOV/SURVIVORS/.

IF MISSING: REPORT OF SEPARATION, DD FORM 214,
COMPLETE: FORM SF-180 AT
WWW.ARCHIVES.GOV/VETERANS.

THE OBITUARY, Template 18

Now is the time to write your own obituary. No one knows you better than you do. At a minimum, write down the key facts about your life on the Living Wish form, Template 17, or complete THE OBITUARY, Template 18, so that your loved ones have all the necessary information to write your obituary. If you would like a picture to accompany your obituary, select your favorite one now and indicate where you keep your favorite photos. The funeral home or your next of kin can submit your obituary to the newspapers that you have specified.

VITAL STATISTICS FORM, Template 19, and DEATH CERTIFICATE

By completing the Vital Statistics Form now, you are providing information that needs to be collected for the death certificate and may not be readily available to your survivors. There are two types of death certificates: those with the cause of death which are used by life insurance companies and beneficiaries; and those without the cause of death for health privacy which are used for public record and title changes for financial institutions, stock brokers, and government agencies.

Your family may need certified death certificates (not copies) in order to file your will for probate; to transfer ownership of stocks, real estate, and automobiles; to change the names on bank accounts; and to apply for benefits from retirement funds, pensions, Social Security, the Veteran's Administration, annuities, and life insurance. Your family can order death certificates from the funeral home or later from the Department of Vital Statistics in the state where the death occurred.

SUMMARY

Now that you have completed your LIVING WISH you have documented how you would like your loved ones to handle the arrangements at your death. Until that time, you can be comforted in knowing that your family knows your wishes.

XIV: PERSONAL LIFE

SAFETY

We do not know how long we will live, but there are things that we can do now to take care of ourselves and live a healthy lifestyle. As we age, hearing, vision, balance, physical capabilities, response time, and memory decline. Personal safety becomes important and there are things that we can do to keep ourselves safe.

A. **EMERGENCY MEDICAL ALERT RESPONSE SYSTEM**

Having seen the advertisements on television showing a woman who has fallen and can't get up, we are aware of the risk of falling as we become unsteady with age. An emergency medical alert response system will enable you to press a button on a wrist band or on a pendant around your neck to summon help. The devices are waterproof so they can be worn in the shower or bathtub. There are many providers of emergency medical alert response systems, such as Life Alert 800-326-1891 and Phillips Lifeline at 800-480-9644 and ADT Medical Alert System at 800-796-0165 that can be found on the Internet or Yellow Pages. MedicAlert + Alzheimer's Association Safe Return provide an ID Bracelet or pendant to be worn by an individual with dementia. Six out of 10 Alzheimer's Disease patients wander, therefore ID jewelry with personalized information and MedicAlert + Safe Return's 24 hour emergency toll-free number identify the individual and their medical conditions and provide a telephone number that can to be called to ensure a safe return of the wanderer. To register with MedicAlert go online to www. medicalert.org/safereturn or call 888-572-8566.

B. **VIAL OF LIFE, Template 20,**

If you call 911 and first responders arrive at your residence, they need important health information about you. You can provide your medical history and medical conditions, the name and telephone number of your doctors, and members of your family who should be contacted in an emergency on a VIAL OF LIFE form, Template 20, which can be obtained online at www.vialoflife. com or by calling 888-724-1200. By keeping this form in a plastic bag taped to your refrigerator door or in your refrigerator at eye level, first responders will have information about you readily available. A Vial of Life sticker at your front door or window advises the first responders to look for the Vial of Life form in the refrigerator upon entry. You may consider placing a copy of your EKG, Living Will, Do Not Resuscitate form, and recent picture of yourself in the plastic bag with your Vial of Life form, Template 20.

C. TIMERS

When it gets dark outside using a timer to turn a light on near your main entrance door, prevents you from entering a dark house and makes your home look occupied to a passer-by.

D. SECURITY MONITORING SYSTEM

A security monitoring system is notified when your residence is entered or broken into by an unauthorized person. When you are in your residence it is wise to have your alarm system activated in "stay" mode so that if a door or window is opened by an intruder, you will be forewarned. You can obtain a pendant from your home security provider to keep by your bed or on your person that you can activate when you hear an intruder or need to contact your security provider for emergency assistance.

If you do not have a security monitoring system in your home there are other techniques you can employ. Keeping your cell phone by your bedside or on your person is also an effective way to call for help in an emergency. Another technique is to keep your car keys by your bed or on your person so that you can press the red emergency button if you hear an intruder or need assistance. The blaring sound from your nearby car may frighten the intruder or cause a neighbor to come to your home to aid you in the case of an emergency.

E. GRAB BARS IN SHOWER AND TOILET AREAS

Don't wait until you are experiencing balance issues to install grab bars in your shower, tub, and toilet areas. It is easy to slip in the shower or tub at any age and often an assist is needed when getting up from the toilet.

F. HANDRAILS ON BOTH SIDES OF STAIRS

The most secure way to go up and down stairs is when you are able to hold on to handrails with both your right and left hands. If you are compromised in your mobility or your hands on either the right or left side, having handrails on both sides, means that you always have one handrail that you can hold on to with your good limb whether ascending or descending the stairs. If you have only one handrail, it is safer to go up and down the stairs sideways, holding on to the handrail with both hands and placing your whole foot on the length of the step and thus avoid falling forwards or backwards.

G. HAND HELD SHOWER HEAD

If you are injured and are not able to take a full body bath or shower, the use of a hand held shower head in the bath tub or shower enables you to bathe yourself while seated on a stool in the tub or shower.

H. SEAT IN SHOWER AND TUB

A built in seat or a plastic stool in the shower or tub makes it possible to bathe when you are not able to put your full body weight on your legs or you cannot lower and/or raise yourself from the floor of the tub.

I. ONE HOME ENTRANCE "RAMP CAPABLE"

Consider which outside door to your residence or door to your garage could accommodate the construction of a ramp to permit wheel chair access to your home when mobility becomes an issue.

J. CARPETS/RUGS WITH SKID PROOF BACKING

Throw rugs that do not have a skid proof backing pose a hazard for slipping or tripping at any age and especially when walking becomes unsteady. Remove throw rugs if there is any movement of the rug or any folding back of the edges.

K. PHONE AND FLASHLIGHT NEAR YOUR BED

Be prepared for unanticipated awakenings at night. Use your flashlight to see the room clearly and have your cell phone or land line nearby so you can call for assistance if you need it.

L. NIGHT LIGHTS IN HALLWAYS AND BATHROOM

It is wise to have your path to the bathroom illuminated at night so if you get up in the night and aren't completely awake you will reduce the risk of falling or bumping into furniture.

M. CLUTTER AND LOOSE ELECTRICAL CORDS

Objects, including small pets, on the floor and loose electrical cords can easily cause a fall especially when you are carrying things which block your vision of the ground. Keep your walkways and floors clear of clutter.

N. HOME SAFETY AND FALL PREVENTION, Template 21

Review the Home Safety and Fall Prevention Checklist, Template 21, to determine if there are some improvements you can make to your home to make it safer and reduce the risk of falling. An unplanned fall can disrupt your lifestyle and often leads to a deterioration in health and attitude.

O. BALANCE CONFIDENCE CHECKLIST, Template 22

Evaluate your balance competence by taking the Balance Confidence (ABC) Scale, Template 22. As our balance declines it is wise to identify those tasks that we perform every day that are becoming more challenging. Often balance training exercises and physical therapy can help to improve balance.

P. GPS (GLOBAL POSITIONING SYSTEM) IN CAR

With age our driving skills may become weakened with declines in judgment, vision, and reflexes. Therefore it is important to be able to keep your eyes focused on the road and be able to anticipate changes in direction. Many cars and smart phones are equipped with Global Positioning Systems (GPS) to provide you with verbal driving instructions as you need them on your way to your destination. This is especially helpful when navigating at night in new areas. If you miss a turn, the GPS gives you immediate instructions to get you back on the correct route. You can save the addresses of frequently used destinations such as the addresses of your home, family, friends, house of worship, grocery store, doctor, pharmacy, restaurants, hospital, and police.

Q. OTHER DRIVERS

Ask a friend for a ride, especially at night, if you are unsure about driving yourself.

R. UNSAFE DRIVERS

As a family member or friend it is difficult to take the keys from someone you believe should no longer be driving. The ability to drive oneself gives one independence and personal freedom that is hard to give up. You can report an unsafe driver anonymously. Check the website of your state's department of highway safety and motor vehicles to obtain the reporting form designed for use by the general public to report medically or physically impaired drivers who may pose a threat to public safety. This report when submitted is confidential and not subject to civil or criminal action against the provider of the information. The form is screened by medical disability specialists and is forwarded to investigators who contact the driver and family members, neighbors, and driver's physician if appropriate.

S. DISABLED PERSON PARKING PERMIT

Apply for a disabled person parking permit from your state department of highway safety and motor vehicles. If you are legally blind or have a disability that limits or impairs your ability to walk, you may apply for a disabled person parking permit. Your physician needs to certify your condition on the application. If you qualify, you will receive a placard to hang from your rear view mirror that will entitle you or your driver to park in a designated disabled person parking space. This space is wider than a normal parking space and is located near the entrance of the building to facilitate getting in and out of the car and to minimize the distance that needs to be walked.

SUMMARY

These are some of the many things that you can do to make your living conditions as safe as possible and minimize the risk of injury to yourself.

BUDGET

By documenting many of the daily activities of our personal life, we can make these tasks easier for ourselves and later for our family members if we become incapacitated or deceased.

FINANCIAL

In each household there is often one person who pays the bills and handles the financial affairs of the family because of aptitude, experience, or interest. If this person becomes incapable of handling the financial matters as a result of illness or death, it is important that the other person in the relationship be able to handle the finances. For this reason an elementary discussion of budgeting and bill payment follows.

BUDGETING

DOCUMENT SOURCES OF INCOME, Template 23

The SCHEDULE OF INCOME form, Template 23, is used to record your monthly income: wages, pension, social security, annuity payments, investment income, and Veteran's benefits. Make a copy of the SCHEDULE OF INCOME form, Template 23, and complete it as follows:

Using information from the income stubs from your employer, pension plan, Social Security Administration, annuity provider, investment firm, and Veteran's Administration, in column 1 of the SCHEDULE OF INCOME form, write the name of the PAYOR who provides the SOURCE OF INCOME. In column 2 indicate the method of receipt: EFT (Electronic Funds Transfer or automatic deposit); CHK (Check); or CASH. In column 3 record the AMOUNT RECEIVED or the average amount received if the amount varies. In column 4 enter the number of payments received per year, for example 12 if monthly, in FREQ PER YEAR. In column 5, enter the date you receive the income in DATE RECEIVED for the income. In column 6 enter the INCOME PER YEAR by multiplying AMOUNT RECEIVED times FREQ PER YEAR. Add up all the INCOME PER YEAR entries and the sum is your TOTAL INCOME FOR THE YEAR.

UPON DEATH

The Executor of your estate will need to contact your employer, pension plan provider, Social Security Administration, annuity provider, and Veteran's Administration to notify them of your death and file for any benefits for your beneficiaries due from these sources. If dividends or distributions were being sent to you or deposited in your bank account, the Executor of your estate will need to notify the institutions that are holding your investments of your death. The applicable date of death values of the investments in your portfolio need to be determined and the assets need to be transferred to an estate account that is created to hold these assets until they are distributed to the designated beneficiaries.

DOCUMENT EXPENSES, Template 24

The SCHEDULE OF PAYMENTS form, Template 24, is used to list the payments that may be fixed or variable in amount that occur WEEKLY, MONTHLY, QUARTERLY, SEMIANNUALLY, ANNUALLY throughout the year. Some of the recurring bills are fixed in amount each month, like monthly membership dues to a fitness center, and others are varied depending on usage, like an electric bill. There are also bills that are varied in amount and frequency which are based on a service provided on a specific date, like a doctor's visit.

The SCHEDULE OF PAYMENTS form, Template 24, can be used to complete the budget for the year. Start by collecting copies of the bills for the current month and any other bills that are paid on intervals (weekly, quarterly, semi-annually, annually) throughout the year. Today there are several ways to pay bills: online bill payment by computer or smart phone; automatic payment (withdrawal) from your checking account by payee (service provider); and paper check. Many people are choosing to go "paperless" and receive their bills online and have the service providers make withdrawals from their checking accounts to pay their bills. For security, banks are enabling their customers to set up "alerts" to notify them when withdrawals or deposits are being made of a certain magnitude. Since each of us has our own comfort level when it comes to convenience and security, the options available are described below but the choice is yours.

There are several ways that you can pay your bills:

ONLINE BILL PAY-- BANK SCHEDULED PAYMENT (BSP)

Online bill payment by computer or smart phone is the option we are currently using. We chose this option because we want to schedule the individual or recurring payments ourselves rather than have service providers automatically deduct payments from our checking account. We like the fact that the bank will trace a payment that a service provider says was not received. We find that we save time and money by not having to write checks ourselves, put them in envelopes, buy stamps, and provide a return address. We currently receive our bills by mail. After paying the bill, we write the check or transaction number and scheduled payment date on the bill and file the bill in a labeled manila folder in a file cabinet drawer for a given year. Entering the payees or service providers in the online bill payment system is a one time job that can be facilitated by using the MEDICAL CONTACTS form, Template 25, and SERVICE PROVIDERS AND FREQUENCY OF SERVICE form, Template 30, which will be described later. These forms have the name, address, and telephone number of the medical contact or service provider, and your account number. When a bill is received for the first time, this information can be added to the online bill payment system when the bill is being paid. For recurring bills of a fixed amount, an automatic repeating bill payment transaction can be set up. Using a smart phone or computer, online inquiries can be made of deposits and withdrawals, scheduled payments, account balances, and payee information. The online bill payment system of many banks offers the capability to download the banking transactions into QUICKEN, a financial software program that can be used to categorize income and expenses to assist in budgeting and the preparation of income tax returns.

PAYEE AUTOMATIC PAYMENT (PAP)

Whether you are using online banking or a manual system to pay your bills, many service providers offer the option of automatically deducting a payment from your checking account when a bill is due. To implement this service, you need to provide the routing number of your bank and your checking account number to the payee along with your authorization.

PAPER CHECK (CHK)

You may prefer to make payments by writing a paper check and mailing it to the service provider by the due date. Deposits, withdrawals, and the current balance can be recorded in a paper check register and balanced with the bank statement.

Most likely you will use a combination of the above techniques to pay your bills and you can indicate on the SCHEDULE OF PAYMENTS (EXPENSES) form, TEMPLATE 24, the technique used for each of your bill payments.

To begin recording your expenses, make multiple copies of the SCHEDULE OF PAYMENTS (EXPENSES) form, TEMPLATE 24. The first copy can be used to list all payments that are weekly and monthly. The second copy can be used to list all payments that are quarterly, semiannually, and annually. The third copy can be used for those payments that are paid as services are received and billed.

Complete each SCHEDULE OF PAYMENTS (EXPENSES) form, TEMPLATE 24, as follows:

Using input from the current bill, in column 1 of the SCHEDULE OF PAYMENTS (EXPENSES) form, TEMPLATE 24, write the name of the PAYEE or service provider. In column 2 indicate the method of payment: BSP (Bank Scheduled Payment), PAP (PAYEE AUTOMATIC PAYMENT), or CHK (Check). In column 3 record the AMOUNT PAID or the average amount paid. In column 4 enter the number of payments per year, for example 12 if monthly, in FREQ PER YEAR. In column 5, enter the DATE PAID for the bill. In column 6 enter the EXPENSE PER YEAR by multiplying the AMOUNT PAID times FREQ PER YEAR. For credit card bills, enter an average monthly payment in AMOUNT PAID.

Add up all the amounts in column 6 (EXPENSE PER YEAR) and the sum of the pages will be your TOTAL EXPENSES FOR THE YEAR. Subtract the TOTAL EXPENSES FOR THE YEAR from the TOTAL INCOME FOR THE YEAR and the result is your net GAIN or LOSS for the year.

Once the SCHEDULE OF PAYMENTS form, TEMPLATE 24, is completed, another person can pick up the list and know what bills to expect and how they are being paid. If a family member becomes incapable of handling his/her financial affairs, another family member or designee can use this list to pay the bills of a loved one and know the yearly expenses that are being incurred to run the household.

UPON DEATH

This SCHEDULE OF PAYMENTS form, Template 24, is helpful for next of kin to determine if there are any automatic bill payments that need to be cancelled upon the death of the family member. This SCHEDULE OF PAYMENTS form, Template 24, can be used to identify the service providers that need to be contacted to remove the name of the deceased from the bills. In the case of the telephone company it is wise to use the first initial and last name of the surviving spouse when changing the listing. The title and registration of all vehicles in the name of the deceased need to be changed. The name of the deceased needs to be removed from the deeds of real estate property. Credit cards in the name of the deceased need to be cancelled and destroyed.

Upon your death, your name needs to be removed from your existing bank accounts. The Executor of your will needs to establish an estate checking account with assets from your checking account which will be used to pay final bills and any bills associated with your death. A detailed accounting of these expenses needs to be submitted to your attorney

MEDICAL

How many times have you been asked: who is your doctor; what is the telephone number of your pharmacy; what surgeries have you had; what medications do you take? The following forms provide you a place where you can enter this information so that you can take these forms with you when you go to a new doctor or are preparing for a hospital procedure. We also keep this information in our smart phones so we always have it with us.

MEDICAL CONTACTS, Template 25

Record the names of all of your doctors with their address, phone number, and your account number on the MEDICAL CONTACTS FORM, Template 25. Include the same information for the pharmacies in your medical plan, local hospitals, and first responders in the case of an emergency. Having this information on one sheet in your SUDDENLY ALONE notebook will be a handy reference when you need to make medical appointments, go to a new doctor, or need to provide this information to a hospital or surgical center prior to admittance. If you decide to implement online bill payment with your bank, this sheet will provide you with all the information you need to easily enter your medical providers into the PAYEE file for future bill payments.

MEDICAL HISTORY: MEDICAL CONDITIONS, SURGERIES AND PROCEDURES, Template 26,

On the MEDICAL HISTORY: MEDICAL CONDITIONS, SURGERIES AND PROCEDURES form, Template 26, list by date all of the surgeries and procedures you have had; dates of your immunizations, such as tetanus shot, shingles shot, flu shot, pneumonia shot; and any allergies you have. Take a copy of this form when you go to the doctor, surgical center or hospital. Keep this information up to date. We also keep this information in our smart phones.

PRESCRIPTIONS AND SUPPLEMENTS, Template 27

Doctors and hospitals always ask for this information, so by completing the PRESCRIPTIONS AND SUPPLEMENTS form, Template 27, you will be able to take a copy of this form and not have to complete the information again when you visit the doctor or have surgery. As more of us are choosing to take supplements in addition to the drugs that are prescribed by our doctors, it is important to have them all listed in one place so that you can review them with your doctor and be able to explain why you are taking them. Your doctor can then describe to you any harmful side effects or possible drug interactions. Keep a copy of the PRESCRIPTIONS AND SUPPLEMENTS form, Template 27, with your VIAL OF LIFE information, TEMPLATE 20, that is in your refrigerator or on the refrigerator door for use in an emergency. We keep this information in our smart phones.

APPOINTMENTS

DOCTOR APPOINTMENTS, Template 28

It is important that we take responsibility for our own health and schedule checkups and necessary tests at recommended intervals. It is helpful to keep a record of your medical appointments on the DOCTOR APPOINTMENTS form, Template 28, listed by frequency per year and the month to be scheduled in order to meet restrictions for coverage by your health care insurance provider. Examples of such routine checkups are:

restrictions for coverage by your health care insurance provider. Examples of such routine checkups are:

> Wellness physical: once a year
> Skin cancer check: twice a year
> Prostate/breast cancer screening: once a year
> Eye exam: once a year
> Hearing test: every 2 years
> Dental cleaning: 2 – 3 times per year
> Visits to specialists as needed

Many doctors schedule your next appointment when you are leaving your current appointment and call to remind you to facilitate this process. We enter all of our future appointments in our smart phones.

OTHER APPOINTMENTS

Besides our responsibility to take care of our bodies in order to live a long and healthy life, it is important to maintain social contacts and strengthen our spirit and mind on a daily basis. According to the Mayo Clinic Health Letter, February 2015, age has little effect on habit-based memory which stores skills that are developed by practice and repetition. We use our smart phone as an extension of our brain, so if we become prone to memory lapses, we have a readily available electronic tool to assist us in finding names, addresses, phone numbers, scheduled events, and to do lists. Plus we can always enter or speak a word or phrase into our smart phone and use a search engine on the phone to answer the question. It is important to select a tool that works for you and use it regularly so that it will become a habit.

SOCIAL CONTACT

One of the best ways to live an active life style is to stay connected to friends, family, and outside organizations. Your personal calendar, whether it is a paper calendar or an electronic one, enables you to be on time and where you should be to maintain your connections with others. We have chosen to schedule our activities on a shared calendar on our smart phones because of the ease of entering and retrieving one-time and recurring events, reminders, directions to locations, attendees, and notes.

Whichever technique you prefer, do the following:

> Enter specific appointments with the date, time, location, and attendees.
> Schedule recurring events, like weekly classes.
> Enter birthdays, anniversaries, and significant events of friends and family.
> Consider scheduling personal time each day for your self-care.
> Check your calendar each night or first thing in the morning so that you won't miss an appointment or event.

DAILY ACTIVITIES

SPIRIT

Having daily quiet time or meditation helps you to stay in the present. You may want to read a daily devotional or religious book to get your day off to a peaceful start.

MIND

The greatest risk factor for Alzheimer's Disease is age. One out of two individuals 85 years or older are afflicted with this memory impairment. Since there is a strong link of Alzheimer's Disease with head injury, we should try to avoid head injury by always wearing a seat belt and fall-proofing our residence. Since our parents had Alzheimer's Disease, our philosophy is to live each day to the fullest and keep our minds active. We rely heavily on our smart phones to keep track of the details of our life. We utilize the calendar function to keep track of all events, past, present, and future and keep information about our friends, family, and service providers in our contacts file. With the search capability of the smart phone we look up people, places, and things with ease.

We keep up on current events by the daily paper, news highlights received on our smart phone, and the nightly news on television. We feel it is important to systematize our daily activities, so that they will become ingrained in our minds, just like brushing our teeth. We endeavor to handle paper only once by taking action on all mail items the day they are received by scheduling an online bill payment for the date due or scheduling the future date of an activity in our smart phone calendar. We have set up a filing system for the paid bills, medical reports, insurance policies, investments, legal papers, and household operations. We file the new item in the appropriate folder the day we receive it to avoid "piles" to be dealt with later ("handle paper once"). Some people choose to scan these documents into their computers to reduce paper files. We write a daily "to do" list for any items that are not scheduled in our smart phone calendar. To avoid stress, we try to be early for appointments and always have reading material from our "read file" with us so waiting is a pleasure not a frustration.

XV: HOUSEHOLD

HOUSEHOLD EQUIPMENT

We used to have a drawer where we placed all of the instruction manuals and service contracts for our household appliances. When we needed to fix something it was a huge job to rummage through the drawer to find the correct information, for example, the part number for the refrigerator water filter. Now we have all of the operation manuals in acetates filed in alphabetical order in 3-ring binders. This has greatly simplified the process for us and will be a handy reference for others when we need assistance.

HOUSEHOLD ITEMS THAT REQUIRE YOUR ATTENTION

By referring to the household equipment operation manuals it is easy to find the information that we need for the care of the following equipment:

AIR CONDITIONER
ANSWERING MACHINE
COMPUTER
COPIER
DISHWASHER
DRYER
DVR
FREEZER
ICE MAKER
LAWN SPRINKLER SYSTEM
MICROWAVE
PRINTER
RANGE
REFRIGERATOR
SECURITY SYSTEM
SMART PHONE
SNOW BLOWER
SWIMMING POOL PUMP AND FILTER
TELEVISION
WASHER
WATER FILTRATION AND/OR WATER SOFTENER SYSTEM

Try operating all of these appliances yourself with supervision from your spouse, a friend, or service provider now. Don't wait until the equipment requires service or you are "suddenly alone."

HOUSEHOLD SAFETY AND MAINTENANCE TO DO ITEMS, Template 29

Develop a checklist of household items that require your attention (replacement, repair, cleaning, inspection) and indicate the frequency of service and the date when this service should be performed. This information should be recorded on the HOUSEHOLD SAFETY AND MAINTENANCE TO DO ITEMS, Template 29.

HOUSEHOLD SERVICE PROVIDERS AND FREQUENCY OF SERVICE, Template 30

Your home is wonderful when everything works. Regularly scheduled maintenance keeps your household equipment performing properly but when repairs are needed it helps to know whom to call. By completing the HOUSEHOLD SERVICE PROVIDERS AND FREQUENCY OF SERVICE form, Template 30, you are prepared for the unexpected. When a friend mentions a service provider whose service was excellent, obtain the name, address, and phone number of the service provider and add this information to your smart phone and/or HOUSEHOLD SERVICE PROVIDERS form, Template 30, for future reference.

HOUSEHOLD SECURITY: UTILITY CONNECTIONS AND KEYS, Template 31

There are many household activities we do easily today but if we were to become incapacitated or deceased, others would need to know how to manage our household and access our personal possessions.

Having had several floods in our homes due to burst water pipes or leaks from toilets or ice makers, we are extremely careful about turning off the water when we leave the house overnight. It is important for all members of the household to know how the utilities are connected to the house and how to keep the house and its contents safe. By completing the HOUSEHOLD SECURITY: UTILITY CONNECTIONS AND KEYS form, Template 31, all family members will be able to know how to keep the house secure.

HOUSEHOLD UTILITY CONNECTIONS

Indicate the location of the water and fuel sources that supply your house and equipment. On the circuit breaker panel and fuse box, clearly label the location in your home that is serviced by the individual circuit breaker or fuse. Circuit breakers that have tripped are in the opposite direction and fuses that have blown are darkened. Have a flash light handy near your circuit breaker panel and/or fuse box, so in the case of a power failure you will be able to see the circuit breaker that has tripped or fuse that needs replacement. Always have spare fuses on hand. If you have a water pump, we recommend turning the circuit breaker that serves the water pump off when you are away. We also turn the circuit breaker off on our water heater when we are going to be away. Another option is to set the thermostat on your water heater to the PILOT setting. Be sure that your family members know how to perform these activities.

SECURITY SYSTEM

We have a security system that is connected to a monitoring company. We alarm the system whenever we leave the house and at night we set the system on STAY so that we will be awakened by an intruder and the monitoring company will be notified and will call the police. In order to arm our security system, a green READY light needs to be on. When the light is not on, some window or door is not closed or a sensor is obstructed. Our security system indicates by number which location in our home has a sensor that is NOT READY. We need to know the number that corresponds to each location. Therefore, we affixed a small piece of paper to the inside of the security system control box, with the numbers of the zones and the area that is serviced by each zone. Now we can easily know which window, door, or electronic beam needs to be corrected in order to put the alarm system in the READY state.

EXTRA HOUSE KEY

It is a good practice to leave a set of keys with a neighbor because inadvertently you may lock yourself out of the house. If you are going to be away from your residence overnight or for an extended period of time, it is wise to advise one of your neighbors who can notify you if something goes wrong. Your neighbor can be your point of contact if your security system goes off. By having a set of keys to your home, your neighbor can unlock your door, so the police will not have to force open the locks to check to see that all is well inside your home. Also if your neighbor notices your newspaper or mail has not been picked up and no one answers the telephone, your neighbor can gain access to your home and check on you in case of a medical emergency. It may also be advisable to leave a spare set of car keys with your neighbor, in the event your car has to be moved while you are away or if you lost your car keys or locked them inside the car while you were away from your home. In the case of a lockout, we obtain the ONSTAR Service telephone number from our smart phone and call ONSTAR to unlock our car via satellite.

SAFE DEPOSIT BOX

If you have chosen to keep your important documents in a bank safe deposit box, a member of your family should know where this key is in order to access your safe deposit box if you are not able. The name and signature of this family member needs to be on file at your bank in order for this person to gain access to your safe deposit box.

UPON DEATH

Bank personnel read the death notices to identify any customers who have died. Upon death, the bank freezes access to the safe deposit box that is in the name of the deceased, and the box cannot be opened until a death certificate is presented. The bank will give access to the safe deposit box to the authorized signers on the box who can remove the contents of the box. If the family member of the deceased does not have a key, it usually takes 1 – 3 business days for a locksmith to drill open the box. To avoid this delay, the family member, who knows where the key is and whose name is on file at the bank, may decide to go to the bank safe deposit box and empty the contents immediately upon the death of the loved one. If no one claims the contents of the box, the bank sends the contents to probate.

LOCATION AND CONTENTS OF SAFE DEPOSIT BOX(ES), Template 32

Complete the LOCATION AND CONTENTS OF SAFE DEPOSIT BOX(ES) form, Template 32, so that members of your family will know where your safe deposit box is located and what items are contained within it. Some people choose to keep their important documents, like copies of their will, trust documents, stocks, bonds, and insurance policies, and valuables, like jewelry and coins in their safe deposit box.

UPON DEATH

It is better to keep the originals of your will and trust documents with your attorney so that they are available sooner to your lawyer and family members upon your death. Likewise it is better to keep your stocks and bonds with a brokerage firm so that upon your death, the brokerage firm can easily change the name on these investments from the name of the decedent to the "estate of" the deceased upon receipt of the death certificate. In most states, if your spouse is the owner of your life insurance policy, the proceeds won't be included in your taxable estate and your beneficiary will have access to the proceeds of the policy once your death certificate is presented. If the beneficiaries are minor children, mentally impaired or elderly adults who cannot manage their own financial affairs, consider placing the proceeds in a trust that is managed for their benefit by the trustee who may be the trust department of a bank. In this way, the money can be dispersed as needed for such things as higher education or health care costs.

CONTENTS OF WALLET: CREDIT CARDS/MEDICAL CARDS/ LICENSES, Template 33

We all dread the thought of losing our purse or wallet because of the important information that it contains. By completing the CONTENTS OF WALLET: CREDIT CARDS/MEDICAL CARDS/LICENSES form, Template 33, you will have in one place all the information you need to contact the issuers of these cards to request that the card be cancelled and a new one be issued. Each year we take all of the cards that we carry around in our purse or wallet and make a copy of the front and back of them for inclusion in our notebook. Each card usually has the telephone number on the back of the card to be used "in case the card is lost or stolen." We also use a credit card registry service so that we can make one telephone call and the credit card registry service will make all of the telephone calls to the issuers of our cards to request cancellation and replacement of our lost cards.

UPON DEATH

Next of kin can use your CONTENTS OF WALLET form, Template 33, to notify the issuers of the cards to cancel the cards of the deceased. The telephone number and website of the card issuer can be found on the copies of the backs of the CREDIT CARDS, MEDICAL CARDS, and LICENSES in your notebook.

COMPUTER NETWORK, Template 34

In this fast paced changing world, it is important to embrace technology. However with each online application that we use comes a website, a user ID, and a user password. We keep all of our passwords in an EXCEL spreadsheet file on our computer and print it. There are software packages that are available to perform the same function. For starters, complete the COMPUTER NETWORK form, Template 34, and list this information for use by family members if they need to access your computer applications when you are not able. Include the location of the CDs and the manuals for the software packages that are installed on your computer.

XVI: LIVING INDEPENDENTLY

Each of us wants to live independently as long as possible. There are things we can do to enhance the quality of our life by living a **HEALTHY LIFESTYLE:**

Activity, Outdoors, Balance, Healthy Meals, Sleep, Stress Relief, Hydration, Personal Connections, Alcohol Moderation, Smoking Cessation, Positive Attitude, Sense of Humor, Support Group.

The risk of developing dementia and osteoporosis increases as we age. One out of two individuals over the age of 85 is likely to develop Alzheimer's Disease. In older adults falls are the leading cause of injuries. By the age of 60 one out of 4 people has the chance of an osteoporosis-related fracture. The following suggestions can help you do your part to increase your chances of living a long and healthy life.

ACTIVITY. Stay active by performing moderately intense physical activity of at least 15 – 30 minutes per day. Vary aerobic and strength training exercises such as: riding a stationary bicycle; using free weights, exercise bands, or an exercise ball. According to the Mayo Clinic Newsletter, February 2015, people who are physically active are less likely to experience a decline in mental function and have a lowered risk of developing Alzheimer's Disease.

OUTDOORS. Get outdoors at least once a day. Walking is one of the best ways to build balance by strengthening your leg muscles. Take a walk if you are able and don't forget the sunscreen and comfortable shoes.

BALANCE. Work on your balance and use a cane if you are unsteady to prevent falls. The Mayo Clinic Newsletter, April 2015 states about three fourths of older Americans have problems with their balance according to the Centers for Disease Control and Prevention. Practice standing on one foot while waiting in the super market checkout lane where you have the handle of your cart to catch you if you become unsteady. Other daily exercises you can try are: while brushing your teeth, stand on one foot; and while talking on the telephone stand with one foot placed in front of the other.

HEALTHY MEALS. Eat a healthy diet of fruits, vegetables, whole grains, and fish. Consider selecting organic fruits and vegetables whenever possible. Review the ENVIRONMENTAL WORKING GROUP'S 2011 SHOPPER'S GUIDE TO

PESTICIDES IN PRODUCE form, Template 35, for guidance on which fruits and vegetables are recommended for organic purchase based on pesticide content.

SLEEP. Try to get a good night's sleep of 7 - 8 hours about the same time every night. While you sleep your body restores itself and you will be more energetic and productive when you awake.

STRESS RELIEF. Minimize stress and learn to relax. Taking deep breaths when under stress can help to calm you. Practicing tai chi and yoga help to slow your breathing while improving your balance and flexibility.

HYDRATION. Drink plenty of water every day. Two thirds of older adults are chronically dehydrated. Dehydration can lead to dizziness and heart palpitations. Water helps to flush the toxins out of your body. If you are properly hydrated, your urine will be clear, not yellow or brownish.

PERSONAL CONNECTIONS. Call or write family members and friends periodically and on their birthday or special occasions.

ALCOHOL MODERATION. Drink alcoholic beverages in moderation. Check with your doctor to learn the amount and type of alcohol that is recommended for your age and health condition. Do not drive after drinking.

SMOKING CESSATION. Talk with your doctor about techniques and support groups that have helped others quit smoking.

POSITIVE ATTITUDE. Keep a gratitude journal by writing down three things you are grateful for each day. A grateful heart protects you from negative thinking and enables you to see the blessings in your life. Change what you can and accept those things you cannot change.

SENSE OF HUMOR. Laughter contributes to health and well-being. Learn to laugh at yourself.

SUPPORT GROUP. There are various twelve step programs and grief share support groups that can assist you in learning tools that helped others get through similar situations successfully.

XVII: WHEN HELP IS NEEDED

When our health declines we need to find others who can assist us. There are many community support services that can be called upon when the need arises.

COMMUNITY SUPPORT SERVICES

A. Meals. Contact your local senior center or search online for names of local services that will deliver meals to your home.

B. Transportation. If you are still able to drive but have mobility issues, contact your state department of motor vehicles for an application for a disabled person parking permit so that you may park your car in the officially designated handicapped parking spaces closer to the entrances of buildings. If you are no longer able to drive, you have several options: local buses which have senior fares and may have wheel chair lifts if needed; special vans for ill or disabled persons; taxi service; rail services with senior fares; and friends who will give you a ride. When you take a ride from a friend, bring along your disabled person parking permit to hang from the mirror.

C. Housekeeping. To locate someone who can assist you by performing housework and meal preparation, you can contact your local senior center or search online for names of local agencies, however personal referrals are best.

D. In-home care. By contacting your local senior center you can obtain the names of agencies that have certified nursing assistants who can help you with the activities of daily living, such as bathing and toileting. You can find the names of local agencies on the internet, but referrals from friends or social workers are best.

E. Activities. Houses of worship, community centers, and senior centers offer fellowship activities for seniors such as lunches at local restaurants and trips to local performances or places of interest.

F. Elder help lines and websites. Contact your local senior center or search online for the support services that you need. Since local support services vary by county and state, the support services listed below are national:

ALZHEIMER'S ASSOCIATION 24 HR. HELPLINE 800-272-3900.

AGENCY FOR HEALTH CARE ADMINISTRATION 888-419-3456.

VA NATIONAL CALL CENTER 800-827-1000.

ELDERCARE LOCATOR 800-677-1116 OR
    WWW.ELDERCARE.GOV
    WWW.ELDERCARE.GOV/ELDERCARE.NET

AREA AGENCIES ON AGING OFFICES AND CONSUMER RESOURCE CENTER
    WWW.N4A.ORG

XVIII: WHEN IT IS TIME TO MOVE

There is no place like home, but due to mental or physical decline living independently in our current home becomes more and more challenging. Since we don't know when we will need to move, it is a good idea to start going through our possessions and disposing of those things which we no longer need. Depending on our physical and mental limitations, it is wise to investigate alternative living arrangements where we can get the assistance we need.

GETTING RID OF "STUFF"

Depending how long you have been living in your residence, you have no doubt accumulated a lot of things. Now that you are preparing to move, this is the time to go through your papers and personal belongings. Besides his book, *It's All Too Much: An Easy Plan For Living a Richer Life with Less Stuff*, written in 2006, Peter Walsh has written several more books on de-cluttering which we also suggest you read. Here are the steps you can follow:

A. As you go through all of your records, consider using this simple technique to handle your papers. Start with a large cardboard box, a box of manila file folders, a marker pen, and a large trash can or shredder. As you review each piece of paper, decide if you are going to keep it or throw it away. If you are keeping the piece of paper, decide on a category for the item, write the category on the tab of the file folder, and file the document in the manila file folder and place the file folder in the cardboard box. Continue to go through your papers and if a manila file folder does not exist for the category of this piece of paper, create a new manila folder and file the folder alphabetically in the cardboard box. For items that you are discarding that contain personal information that could expose you to identity theft, you can shred them yourself or use a professional shredding service.

B. Go through your residence and take pictures or video all of your furniture, jewelry, antiques, art, and other furnishings. If there are any memories or family stories associated with these items, now is the time to write them down or record them with the pictures on your smart phone.

C. Identify the items in each room that you want to keep and write them down or record them in a computer spreadsheet so that you can give this list to the moving company when you are ready to get an estimate of the cost of the move. Make columns for ITEM NUMBER, DESCRIPTION, PICTURE NUMBER, FROM ROOM in your current residence, TO ROOM in your new residence, and BOX NUMBER when the item is packed.

D. Create a computer or manual spreadsheet of all the items that you want to give away. Make columns for ITEM NUMBER, DESCRIPTION, PICTURE NUMBER, FROM ROOM and TO PERSON. You can send copies of this spreadsheet to family members and friends so they can let you know if they would like any of your items. It meant a great deal to us to receive items from our parents before they passed away, so that we could learn the history associated with the items and share with them our enjoyment in having the items, such as a necklace and silver tea service.

E. You may have already made decisions about items that you want to give to specific family members or friends upon your death. If so, review your "SPECIFIIC LIST OF ASSETS - OTHER-- ALL OTHER ASSETS (JEWELRY, FINE ARTS, ETC.)," TEMPLATE 10. Add any items you have omitted and delete any items that you have disposed of.

F. For remaining items contact local charities and thrift shops who will give you a "donation receipt" and may pick up your donations. If you would like to sell your items, consider having a garage sale; taking your items to consignment shops; or listing your items for online sale on sites like www.craigslist.com or www.ebay.com. If you have a large number of items, you may decide it is best to hire a professional to hold an estate or house sale.

SELLING YOUR HOUSE OR CONDO

Ask your friends for names of successful realtors in your area. Some real estate agents are "elder specialists." Elder Life Financial Services at 888-228-4500 can offer you a line of credit until you sell your house or condo. This is helpful as it may be difficult to sell your property before it is time to move into your new facility.

PREPARING TO MOVE

A. Make a floor plan of your new location using graph paper and measurements.

B. Make a scale drawing of the furniture you want to place in each room using your computer or manual spreadsheet. Placing the paper furniture pieces on the paper floor plan is a lot easier than moving the furniture around after it is delivered.

C. Obtain packing supplies online or from a nearby do-it-yourself moving company, like U-Haul.

D. If you decide to do some of the packing yourself, number each box as you pack it and note the number on your computer or manual spreadsheet. If you use a moving company to pack your items, you can specify the way you would like the items to be packed and the way boxes should be marked, for example by room or item type.

E. Make a list of the contents of each box or update your computer or manual spreadsheet with the box number in which the item was placed.

F. Mark each box with the room where the contents of the box will go.

ALTERNATIVE LIVING ARRANGEMENTS

There are many factors that cause you to consider moving from your home to an alternative living arrangement. They include: mobility issues; failing eyesight; memory impairment; personal care needs (toileting, feeding, transfer to/from chair and bed); administration of medications; meal preparation assistance; housekeeping; requirements and cost for indoor and outside building maintenance and repair; safety issues; inability to drive oneself; need for supervision; and desire for social interaction. Since you probably don't want to move again, it is important to become familiar with the alternative living offerings in your area or near family members before the need to move arises. Discuss the subject with your family and friends; visit nearby facilities; write down features that are important to you; consider your immediate and long term needs, your geographical preference, and the costs for basic services and additional services you may need in the future.

OPTIONS FOR ALTERNATIVE LIVING

A. Staying put. We all want to stay in our home as long as possible, but to do this we need a community of peers who support each other or services in the community that we can pay for as we need them.

B. Life Care Communities or Continuing Care Communities. These communities require an upfront investment and have a monthly service fee. The residents need to meet financial, physical, and mental criteria in order to move into Independent Living (IL). When the resident can no longer live on his or her own and needs some assistance with the activities of daily living, the resident may be moved to Assisted Living (AL) if available or may need to pay for needed services in his/her residence. If these options are not available, then the resident if memory impaired may be moved to Memory Care (MC) or Skilled Nursing (SN) or Rehabilitation (RH) if an acute situation has occurred.

C. Adult Rental Communities. These communities usually do not require an upfront investment as monthly rental is used as payment for services. The monthly rental is based on the level of service used. Sometimes there is a monthly fee for additional items like pet fee, community fee, etc. Adult Rental Communities may offer Independent Living (IL), Assisted Living (AL), Skilled Nursing (SN), Rehabilitation (RH), and/or Memory Care (MC).

D. Nursing Centers. Monthly fees are charged based on the type of care provided. The type of care provided includes Skilled Nursing (SN), Rehabilitation (RH), Memory Care (MC) and/or Long Term Care (LTC).

E. Hospice Care. When one has a life-limiting illness, usually six months or less one can utilize Hospice Care either in one's residence or at a Hospice facility. Most insurance companies, Medicare, and Medicaid will pay benefits for these services.

LONG TERM CARE INSURANCE

We strongly urge you to consider long term care insurance with our increasing life span and the increasing costs of care for long term illness. There are many types of long term care insurance with a wide range of costs depending on your age when you procure the policy and the type of coverage you desire. We were fortunate to obtain a group plan long term care insurance policy offered through our employer when we were in our late forties. Parents of employees could apply as well, so my mother signed up for her policy at age 78. In order to obtain long term care insurance the applicant needs to meet the medical requirements of the insurance company. For example my stepfather, who had been successfully treated for prostate cancer within the past five years of his application, did not qualify.

Factors to be considered when selecting your coverage include:

> Maximum Daily Amount for Nursing Home Care
> Maximum Daily Amount for Alternative Care Facility Care
> Maximum Daily Amount for Home Health Care/Adult Day Care
> Maximum Daily Amount for Informal Care
> Calendar Year Maximum For Informal Care
> Lifetime Maximum Benefit

Over the life of the policy, the insurance company may have cost of living premium increases and/or offer upgrades that may increase the lifetime maximum benefit (if there is one) or offer additional coverage options for an additional monthly cost. Once the policy holder is "certified" as needing assistance in a specific number of the activities of daily living, such as toileting, bathing, dressing, eating, transferring to/from bed, incontinence, or memory impairment, a waiting period, for example 90 days, begins. After the waiting period is completed, the policy holder's premium is usually waived and reimbursement up to the maximum daily amount begins. The monthly reimbursements continue until the lifetime maximum, if there is one stipulated in the policy, is reached. This maximum is often about 5 years, but varies with the terms of the policy, the maximum daily amount and the type of care provided.

For individuals who would like long term care insurance but cannot afford the premiums nor meet the medical requirements, there are two types of hybrid policies: annuity-type policies and life insurance policies that contain a long term care rider. A one-time lump sum payment is paid at the inception of the annuity-type policies and most of the life insurance-type policies. If you do not file any claims on the annuity-type policy, you may be able to cash in the policy or upon death be eligible for a return of most of the premium. In the case of a life insurance policy with a long term care rider, if you do not file a claim, you will be entitled to a death benefit that is greater than the premium on the life-insurance-type policy.

It is important to check with the facility you are considering to determine if the benefits provided by your long term care policy can be applied to the cost of services that you will utilize in the residence now or in the future.

CONCLUSION

It is our hope that the information presented in this book will assist you in documenting the many aspects of your life and in planning for a long and healthy future.

SECTION III:

TEMPLATES TO BE COMPLETED BY YOU

PERSONAL INFORMATION TEMPLATES:

A: KEY ADVISORS

B: RELATIVES AND CLOSE FRIENDS

C: PERSONAL IDENTIFICATION DOCUMENTS

D: GENERAL INFORMATION

E: MISCELLANEOUS INFORMATION

F: IMPORTANT THINGS

A: KEY ADVISORS TO BE CONTACTED:

ACCOUNTANT: _____

Phone: _____ **Firm:** _____

Address: _____

ATTORNEY: _____

Phone: _____

Address: _____

AUTO INSURANCE AGENT: _____

Phone: _____ **Firm:** _____

Address: _____

BANK: _____

Phone: _____ **Firm:** _____

Address: _____

CLERGY: _____

Phone: _____ **Church/Synagogue:** _____

Address: _____

DOCTOR: _____

Phone: _____ **Hospital:** _____

Address: _____

EMPLOYER: _____

Phone: _____ **Firm:** _____

Address: _____

FINANCIAL ADVISOR:_____

Phone:_____ **Firm** _____

Address: _____

FUNERAL DIRECTOR:_____

Phone: _____ **Firm:** _____

Address: _____

GENERAL INSURANCE AGENT: _____

Phone:_____ **Firm** _____

Address: _____

LANDLORD:_____

Phone:_____ **Firm** _____

Address _____

LIFE INSURANCE AGENT:_____

Phone:_____ **Firm** _____

Address _____

PARTNER: _____

Phone:_____ **Firm** _____

Address _____

STOCKBROKER: _____

Phone:_____ **Firm** _____

Address _____

TRUST OFFICER:_____

Phone:_____ **Institution** _____

Address _____

B: RELATIVES AND CLOSE FRIENDS TO BE CONTACTED (BE SURE TO MAKE MULTIPLE COPIES OF THIS SPECIFIC TEMPLATE TO CONTAIN ALL OF YOUR RELATIVES AND FRIENDS)

NAME _____

Relationship _____ Phone _____

Address: _____

NAME _____

Relationship _____ Phone _____

Address: _____

NAME _____

Relationship _____ Phone _____

Address: _____

NAME _____

Relationship _____ Phone _____

Address: _____

NAME _____

Relationship _____ Phone _____

Address: _____

NAME _____

Relationship _____ Phone _____

Address: _____

NAME _____

Relationship _____ Phone _____

Address: _____

C: PERSONAL IDENTIFICATION DOCUMENTS: (List each item and where the original is located and make a copy of each to be inserted here).

This is the section where you record your personal identification documents information including a copy of each document to be included (several should fit on one copy page). Be sure to note here where the original of each of these documents is located. Make as many separate copy pages as you need to collect all of your Personal Identification documents.

Below is a sample listing of personal identification documents:

DOCUMENTS: _____ WHERE LOCATED: _____

- **LICENSES**
  - ○ **DRIVERS** _____
  - ○ **PROFESSIONAL** _____
  - ○ **FISHING/HUNTING** _____
- **PASSPORTS** _____
- **PERMITS**
  - ○ **CONCEALED WEAPONS** _____
  - ○ **OTHER** _____
- **MEMBERSHIPS/ASSOCIATIONS**
  - ○ **CLUBS** _____
  - ○ **AAA** _____
  - ○ **AARP** _____
  - ○ **OTHER** _____

D: GENERAL INFORMATION TEMPLATE:

Much of your important information would fit into this "General Information" category. Those listed below are just a sample of what you may have.

Section E: "Personal Information" also contains important Personal legal documents such as Birth Certificates, Marriage License, Military Records, Social Security Cards, etc.

The primary purpose of both of these templates is to contain in one place the locations of your important documents.

My safe deposit box is located at:_____

The keys to the safe deposit box are located at:_____

My personal safe is located at: _____

My tax records are located at: _____

E: PERSONAL INFORMATION:
(Keep copies of the following documents in this book):

Birth certificate: Original located at: _____

Marriage license: Original located at: _____

Military Records: Original located at: _____

Social Security Card: Original located at: _____

Judgments from any court cases affecting me (e.g. divorce, etc.) are located at: _____

F: IMPORTANT THINGS:

Estate Documents (DPOA, LIVING TRUST, HEALTH CARE DPOA, HIPAA RELEASE, LIVING WILL, DNR, WILL, LETTER OF INSTRUCTION):

_____

Past Income Tax Returns: _____

Divorce/Separation papers: _____

Adoption papers: _____

Death Certificates: _____

Citizenship papers: _____

Passports: _____

Leases/Mortgages: _____

Instructions Upon Death _____

Family Albums: _____

Autobiography or family tree/history: _____

Favorite photos: _____

BANK ASSETS, TEMPLATE 1

KEEP A COPY OF CERTIFICATES OF DEPOSIT IN THIS BOOK.

It would be helpful to successor trustee(s) if this list is kept up-to-date.

LOCATION OF ORIGINALS: _____

ALL BANK ACCOUNTS INCLUDE CHECKING, SAVINGS, CD'S, ETC.		

NAME AND ADDRESS OF INSTITUTION	TYPE OF ACCOUNT	ACCOUNT NUMBER

KEN and DONNA WRIGHT

INVESTMENT ASSETS, TEMPLATE 2

KEEP A COPY OF BROKERAGE INFORMATION IN THIS BOOK

LOCATION OF ORIGINALS _____

ALL BROKERAGE ACCOUNTS		

NAME OF BROKERAGE FIRM	NAME AND ADDRESS OF BROKER	ACCOUNT NUMBER

STOCKS, TEMPLATE 3
KEEP A COPY OF STOCK CERTIFICATES & DIVIDEND REINVESTMENTS IN BOOK

LOCATION OF ORIGINALS: _____

ALL STOCK CERTIFICATES AND DIVIDEND REINVESTMENTS HELD INDIVIDUALLY (THOSE NOT WITH A BROKER)

NAME OF CORPORATION	NAME AND ADDRESS OF TRANSFER AGENT	CERTIFICATE NUMBER

MUTUAL FUNDS, TEMPLATE 4
KEEP A COPY OF MUTUAL FUND INFORMATION IN THIS BOOK

LOCATION OF ORIGINALS _____

ALL MUTUAL FUNDS HELD INDIVIDUALLY (THOSE NOT WITH A BROKER)		
NAME OF MUTUAL FUND COMPANY	**NAME AND ADDRESS OF COMPANY**	**ACCOUNT NUMBER**

BONDS, TEMPLATE 5
KEEP A COPY OF BONDS IN THIS BOOK

LOCATION OF ORIGINALS: _____

ALL BONDS HELD INDIVIDUALLY (THOSE NOT WITH A BROKER)		

TYPE OF BOND	NAME AND ADDRESS OF AGENT TO CONTACT	BOND/ACCOUNT NUMBER

ACCOUNTS RECEIVABLE, TEMPLATE 6

KEEP A COPY OF ALL NOTES, MORTGAGES, CREDITOR CONTRACTS, ETC. IN THIS BOOK

LOCATION OF ORIGINALS _____

ALL ACCOUNTS RECEIVABLE

NAME AND ADDRESS OF DEBTOR	DUE DATE OF PAYMENT	SECURITY FOR DEBT

BUSINESS ASSETS, TEMPLATE 7

KEEP COPIES OF EVIDENCE OF ANY BUSINESS ASSETS AND AGREEMENTS IN THIS BOOK (e.g., Partnership agreements, Buy-Sell agreements, closed corporation stock certificates, and miscellaneous business agreements)

LOCATION OF ORIGINALS _____

ALL BUSINESS ASSETS

TYPE OF ASSET	LOCATION OF ASSET	ACCOUNT OR ID NUMBER

<u>REAL ESTATE, TEMPLATE 8</u>

KEEP COPIES OF ALL DEEDS IN THIS BOOK (REVIEW HOW THEY ARE TITLED)

LOCATION OF ORIGINALS _____

ALL REAL ESTATE	

ADDRESS OF PROPERTY	TYPE OF PROPERTY

TITLED PROPERTY, TEMPLATE 9

KEEP COPIES OF TITLES IN THIS BOOK (REVIEW HOW THEY ARE TITLED)

LOCATION OF ORIGINALS _____

ALL TITLED PROPERTY INCLUDE CARS, TRUCKS, CAMPERS, BOATS, MOTORCYCLES, MOBILE HOMES, ETC.

YEAR	MAKE	MODEL	STATE WHERE TITLED

KEN and DONNA WRIGHT

OTHER ASSETS, TEMPLATE 10

ALL OTHER ASSETS
(JEWELRY, FINE ARTS, ETC.)

SCHEDULE OF TAX-DEFERRED IRA'S, TEMPLATE 11

INCLUDE COPIES OF THE FACE PAGE OF POLICIES, AGREEMENTS, ETC.

LOCATION OF ORIGINALS _____

IRA'S	COMPANY	BENEFICIARY DESIGNATIONS PRIMARY	CONTINGENT

SCHEDULE OF TAX-DEFERRED ANNUITIES, TEMPLATE 12

INCLUDE COPIES OF THE FACE PAGE OF POLICIES, AGREEMENTS, ETC.

LOCATION OF ORIGINALS _____

TAX DEFERRED ANNUITIES	COMPANY	BENEFICIARY DESIGNATIONS	
		PRIMARY	CONTINGENT

SCHEDULE OF TAX-DEFERRED INVESTMENTS, TEMPLATE 13

INCLUDE COPIES OF THE FACE PAGE OF POLICIES, AGREEMENTS, ETC.

LOCATION OF ORIGINALS _____

	COMPANY	BENEFICIARY DESIGNATIONS	
		PRIMARY	CONTINGENT

PENSION			
PROFIT SHARING			
OTHER			

SCHEDULE OF OTHER INCOME, TEMPLATE 14

INCLUDE COPIES OF THE FACE PAGE OF POLICIES, AGREEMENTS, ETC.

LOCATION OR ORIGINALS: _____

	ACCOUNT #	BENEFICIARY DESIGNATIONS	
		PRIMARY	CONTINGENT

SOCIAL SECURITY			
INTEREST			
DIVIDENDS			

INSURANCE, TEMPLATE 15

SCHEDULE OF LIFE INSURANCE/NON TAX-DEFERRED ANNUITIES.

INCLUDE COPIES OF THE FACE PAGE OF INSURANCE POLICIES.

LOCATION OF ORIGINALS _____

COMPANY AND POLICY NUNBER	PERSON INSURED	PRIMARY DESIGNATIONS PRIMARY CONTINGENT
LIFE INSURANCE		
NON TAX-DEFERRED ANNUITES		

<u>SCHEDULE OF OTHER TYPES OF INSURANCE, TEMPLATE 16</u>

HAVE COPIES OF THE FACE PAGE OF YOUR INSURANCE POLICIES.

LOCATION OF ORIGINAL _____

POLICY NUMBER	COMPANY	AMOUNT AND TYPE OF BENEFITS
DISABILITY		
MEDICAL		
AUTO		
HOMEOWNERS		
WINDSTORM		
UMBRELLA		
FLOOD		
OTHER LIABILITY		
OTHER		

SECTION III: SELF-CARE TEMPLATES

A LIVING WISH, TEMPLATE 17

THE FOLLOWING ARE MY INSTRUCTIONS FOR EVENTS FOLLOWING MY PHYSICAL DEATH:

A. NOTIFY THE FUNERAL DIRECTOR AND CLERGY AT ONCE.

B. FUNERAL DIRECTOR TO BE CALLED: _____

C. CLERGY TO BE CALLED: _____

D. HAVE BODY HANDLED IMMEDIATELY IN FASHION INDICATED BELOW.

E. PLAN SERVICE WITH CLERGY.

F. NOTIFY THE FOLLOWING: (LAWYER, FAMILY, CLOSE FRIENDS).

_____

_____

_____

_____

_____

THE CARE OF MY BODY:

A. I PREFER THAT MY BODY BE BURIED _____ CREMATED _____
   IF BURIED, I PREFER _____ CEMETERY
   I NOW OWN A LOT IN _____ CEMETERY
   IF CREMATION, THE ASHES SHOULD BE _____

B. I HAVE PREVIOUSLY GIVEN PERMISSION FOR (EYES, KIDNEY, BODY, ETC.) TO BE TURNED OVER TO THE FOLLOWING MEDICAL AUTHORITY (PLEASE DESIGNATE): _____

_____

C. EMBALMING: _____ YES   MINIMIMUM REQUIRED BY LAW _____

D. COFFIN: SIMPLE AS POSSIBLE _____ AVERAGE _____ UP TO FAMILY _____
VAULT: NO _____ (OR MINIMUM REQUIRED BY CEMETERY), YES _____ KIND ___

THE SERVICE:

A. TO BE HELD AT: HOUSE OF WORSHIP ___ **FUNERAL HOME** ___ **OTHER:** ___

B. SCRIPTURAL PASSAGES I WOULD LIKE INCLUDED:

_____

_____

_____

C. MUSICAL SELECTIONS: _____

_____

_____

D. OTHER THOUGHTS ABOUT THE SERVICE: _____

_____

_____

_____

E. THE PHYSICAL BODY: NOT TO BE AT SERVICE: _____ **AT SERVICE** _____

SPECIAL WISHES IN THIS MANNER: _____

_____

_____

F. FLOWERS: TYPE REQUESTED: _____
NO SPECIAL WISHES _____ **NOTICE TO READ:**
"In lieu of flowers, donations may be made to: _____

A MEMORIAL:

I UNDERSTAND THAT NO MEMORIAL IS NECESSARY NOR REQUESTED. IF SURVIVORS WISH TO DO SO, I WOULD PREFER: _____

_____

OTHER WISHES: _____

_____

_____

NAME: _____ **DATE:** _____

HERE IS MY OBITUARY OR KEY FACTS ABOUT MY LIFE:

_____

_____

_____

_____

_____

_____

_____

_____

_____

_____

_____

_____

_____

_____

_____

_____

_____

_____

_____

_____

_____

_____

_____

MY FAVORITE PHOTOS ARE LOCATED IN: _____

THE OBITUARY, TEMPLATE 18

We will submit an obituary to any newspaper in the country you or your loved ones wish and have them contact and bill you directly. Completing the following form will assist with preparing the obituary.

_____ of _____, died
(Name of deceased)   (City, State of residence)

_____ at the age of _____ years. _____was
(Date of death)   (age)

born _____in _____.
              (given name)   (City, State, or Foreign Country)

Activities and hobbies enjoyed: _____

_____

_____

Take time to write a few words of your own: _____

_____

_____

_____

Survivors: Name	Relationship	City/State

Grand of: _____ Great Grand of: _____ Great-Great Grand of: _____

_____

Services:

Date: _____ Time: _____ Place: _____

Address: _____ City: _____

Contributions may be made to (please include address):_____

_____

Contact Person: _____ Telephone: _____

Relationship: _____

From: The Neptune Society: Cremation Planning & Information Book

VITAL STATISTICS FORM, TEMPLATE 19

This form is used to file the death certificate. It should be completed by you since it contains information that could be difficult for loved ones to compile.

First Name: _____ Middle Name: _____

Last Name: _____ Social Security Number: _____

Date of Birth: _____ Birthplace: _____ Sex: _____
(City & State or Foreign Country)

Primary Occupation (before retirement): _____ Years in Practice: _____

Kind of Industry or Business: _____

Married, Never Married, Widowed, Divorced, Married but Separated (specify): _____

Name of Spouse (use maiden name): _____ (Spouse deceased? Yes/No) _____

Usual Residence Street Address: _____

City or Town: _____ State: _____ Zip: _____

County: _____ Phone: _____ Years in County: _____

Father's name (first, middle, last): _____ Father's State of Birth: _____

Mother's name (first, middle, last): _____ Mother's State of Birth: _____

Highest Grade Completed in School: _____

If Veteran: Date of Enlistment: _____ Place of Enlistment: _____

Date of Discharge: _____ Place of Discharge: _____

Serial Number: _____ Rate or Rank: _____

Branch of Service: _____

Immediate Next of Kin: _____ Email Address: _____

Relationship _____ Telephone #: _____

Street Address: _____

City: _____ State: _____ Zip: _____

Do you have annuities? _____ Do you have life insurance: _____

From: The Neptune Society: Cremation Planning & Information Book

VIAL OF LIFE, TEMPLATE 20

Date Completed _____

VIALOFLIFE.com   1-888-724-1200

FIRST NAME	INITIAL	LAST NAME	SOCIAL SECURITY NUMBER
STREET	CITY	STATE ZIP	TELEPHONE

DATE OF BIRTH	MALE/FEMALE	HEIGHT	WEIGHT	HAIR COLOR	EYE COLOR	BLOOD TYPE	RELIGION

List hearing difficulties

List vision difficulties

DENTURES
UPPER LOWER

UNABLE TO SPEAK ☐

NATIVE LANGUAGE IF NOT ENGLISH

Identifying Marks

Current Medical Conditions

Past Medical Conditions

Current Medications: Dosage and Frequency

Allergies to Medications

Doctors Name and Telephone Number

Last Hospitalization

Special Instructions such as health directives, etc...

Health Insurance Policy

Emergency Contact Notification - Name - Address - Phone - Relationship

69-A

PLACE ON REFRIGERATOR DOOR - PLEASE PRINT CLEARLY

HOME SAFETY & FALL PREVENTION CHECKLIST TEMPLATE 21

Gordon College Center for Balance and Mobility
255 Grapevine Road, Wenham, MA
978 867-4095

Home Safety and Fall Prevention Checklist

Client Name: _____   Date: _____

Address: _____

_____   Evaluated by: _____

General Safety Recommendations:

Do you wear supportive, rubber-soled, low heeled shoes? Avoid shoes with thick treads.

Do slippers fit well and have soles that provide traction? Avoid walking in stocking feet.

Do you rise slowly from sitting and pause before you begin to walk?

Do you move slowly when turning or changing direction?

Do you avoid rushing to answer the door or phone?

Do you avoid multiple tasks? Attend to walking first.

When carrying items do you make sure they do not block your view? Avoid carrying bulky items in two hands.

Do you divide large loads into smaller loads leaving one hand free to grasp the railing? If you use a cane avoid carrying items while ascending and descending stairs.

Do you always use a step stool with handles, never a chair when reaching high places?

Are you alert to unexpected hazards in your path, such as out of place toys, furniture or pets?

Do you use a cane or walking stick to compensate for lack of sensation in your feet?

Do you use a cane or walker if you feel unsteady?

Are you alert as you enter or exit areas that have curbs?

Proper Lighting

Do you turn on lights before entering a room?

Do you have night lights in hallways, bathrooms and bedrooms?

Are outdoor walkways properly lit at night?

Secure Walkways

Is carpeting securely fastened down? Avoid scatter rugs or plush carpeting.

Are walkways kept clear of things that could trip you such as phone or extension cords, papers or clutter? Keep walkways clear of miscellaneous or misplaced objects.

Stairways

Is there a light switch at the top and bottom of stairs?

Can you clearly see the outline of each step as you go down the stairs? If not place bright tape at the edge of each tread.

Do all stairways have sturdy handrails that extend slightly beyond the steps?

Are stair coverings securely fastened and free from tears or holes?

Are steps in good repair (not loose or broken, missing or worn?)

Kitchen

Are your floors non-skid?

Do floor mats have non-skid backing?

Can you reach things you use most often without using a step stool or reaching over head.

Bathroom

Does your shower or tub have non-skid surface?

Do you use a shower chair or bench if you are unsteady standing? Use a hand held shower.

Do you have and use well fastened grab bars in tub/shower and on the wall next to the tub/shower?

Can you get on/off the toilet easily? Use a raised toilet seat or grab bar for greater ease if necessary.

Is the floor safe with non-skid tile, secure bath mats or rugs?

Bedroom

Do you have a light or flashlight within easy reach of your bed?

Do you have and use a night light that lights your way to the bathroom?

Is there a phone within reach of your bed?

Modifications recommended to help prevent a fall:

1. _____

_____

2. _____

_____

3. _____

_____

4. _____

_____

Therapist Signature _____ Date: _____

BALANCE CONFIDENCE (ABC) SCALE, TEMPLATE 22

Balance Confidence (ABC) Scale

For <u>each</u> of the following activities, please indicate your level of self-confidence by choosing a corresponding number from the following rating scale:

0% 10% 20% 30% 40% 50% 60% 70% 80% 90% 100%

No   Completely

Confidence   Confident

"How confident are you that you can maintain your balance and remain steady when you………

1. walk around the house? _____%

2. walk up or down stairs? _____%

3. bend over and pick up a slipper from the front of a closet floor? _____%

4. reach for a small can off a shelf at eye level? _____%

5. stand on your tip toes and reach for something above your head? _____%

6. stand on a chair and reach for something? _____%

7. sweep the floor? _____%

8. walk outside the house to a car parked in the driveway? _____%

9. get into or out of a car? _____%

10. walk across a parking lot to the mall? _____%

11. walk up or down a ramp? _____%

12. walk in a crowded mall where people rapidly walk past you? _____%

13. are bumped into by people as you walk through the mall? _____%

14. step onto or off of an escalator while holding onto a railing? _____%

15. step onto or off an escalator while holding onto parcels such that you cannot hold onto the railing? _____%

16. walk outside on icy sidewalks? _____%

Anita M. Myers. Dept of Health Studies & Gerontology. University of Waterloo. Waterloo, Ontario, Canada N2L 3G1.

FINANCIAL: <u>SCHEDULE OF INCOME, TEMPLATE 23</u>

SOURCE OF INCOME	EFT/ CHK/ CASH	AMOUNT RECEIVED	FREQ PER YEAR	DATE RECEIVED	INCOME PER YEAR

EFT= ELECTRONIC FUNDS   1 = ONCE
   TRANSFER (DEPOSIT)   2 = TWICE
  CHK=CHECK   4 = QUARTERLY
                            12 = MONTHLY
                            52 = WEEKLY

FINANCIAL: SCHEDULE OF PAYMENTS (EXPENSES), TEMPLATE 24

PAYEE	BSP/ PAP/ CHK	AMOUNT PAID	FREQ PER YEAR	DATE PAID	EXPENSE PER YEAR
TOTAL YEARLY EXPENSES					

BSP=BANK SCHEDULED (BILL) PAYMENT (MANUAL OR REPEATING)
PAP=PAYEE AUTOMATIC (BILL) PAYMENT (DEDUCTION)

1 = ONCE
2 = TWICE
4 = QUARTERLY
12 = MONTHLY
52 = WEEKLY

KEN and DONNA WRIGHT

MEDICAL CONTACTS, TEMPLATE 25

MEDICAL DOCTORS:	ADDRESS	PHONE #	ACCOUNT #
PHARMACIES:			
HOSPITALS:			
EMERGENCY:			
POLICE			
FIRE			

MEDICAL HISTORY: CONDITIONS, SURGERIES AND PROCEDURES, TEMPLATE 26

DOCTOR	SPECIALTY	PROCEDURE	DATE
IMMUNIZATIONS:			
ALLERGIES:			

MEDICAL: PRESCRIPTIONS AND SUPPLEMENTS, TEMPLATE 27

DRUG NAME	DOSAGE	FREQUENCY	REASON

SUPPLEMENT	DOSAGE	FREQUENCY	BRAND NAME

DOCTOR APPOINTMENTS, TEMPLATE 28

DOCTOR	REASON	FREQUENCY	DATE OF VISIT

HOUSEHOLD SAFETY AND MAINTENANCE TO DO ITEMS, TEMPLATE 29

HOUSEHOLD TASK	FREQUENCY	DATE TO BE DONE

HOUSEHOLD SERVICE PROVIDERS & FREQUENCY OF SERVICE, TEMPLATE 30

NAME OF PROVIDER	ADDRESS	PHONE #	ACCOUNT#	FREQ

HOUSEHOLD SECURITY: UTILITY CONNECTIONS AND KEYS, TEMPLATE 31

HOUSEHOLD UTILITY CONNECTION	LOCATION OF UTILITY CONNECTION
MAIN HOUSEHOLD WATER TURN OFF	
SPRINKLER/HOSE WATER TURN OFF	
WATER FILTRATION/SOFTENER SYSTEM TURN OFF	
SWIMMING POOL PUMP/FILTRATION SYSTEM TURN OFF	
GAS TURN OFF	
REFRIGERATOR WATER TURN OFF	
ICE MAKER TURN OFF	
CIRCUIT BREAKER BOX OR FUSE BOX LABEL EACH BREAKER OR FUSE	
SECURITY SYSTEM CONTROL BOX LABEL EACH ZONE	
LOCATION OF SPARE HOUSE KEYS	
LOCATION OF SAFE DEPOSIT KEY	

LOCATION AND CONTENTS OF SAFE DEPOSIT BOX(ES), TEMPLATE 32

LOCATION OF SAFE DEPOSIT BOX(ES):

ITEMS IN SAFE DEPOSIT BOX(ES):

CONTENTS OF WALLET: CREDIT AND MEDICAL CARDS/LICENSES, TEMPLATE 33

CARD NAME	CARDHOLDER NAME	CARD NUMBER	EXPIRE DATE	SEC CODE
CREDIT CARD				
MEDICAL				
LICENSES				

COMPUTER NETWORK, TEMPLATE 34

WEBSITE NAME	WEBSITE URL	USER ID	PASSWORD

SOFTWARE CD'S AND THEIR LOCATIONS:

_____

_____

_____

_____

OWNER'S MANUALS AND THEIR LOCATIONS:

_____

_____

_____

_____

WHEN TO EAT ORGANIC, TEMPLATE 35

Environmental Working Group's 2011 Shopper's Guide to Pesticides in Produce™

DIRTY DOZEN™

Buy these organic: worst (*)

1. Apples*
2. Celery*
3. Strawberries*
4. Peaches
5. Spinach
6. Nectarines (Imported)
7. Grapes (Imported)
8. Sweet bell peppers
9. Potatoes
10. Blueberries (Domestic)
11. Lettuce
12. Kale/collard greens

CLEAN FIFTEEN™

Lowest in Pesticides: best (*)

1. Onions*
2. Corn*
3. Pineapples*
4. Avocado
5. Asparagus
6. Sweet peas
7. Mangoes
8. Eggplant
9. Cantaloupe (Domestic)
10. Kiwi
11. Cabbage
12. Watermelon
13. Sweet potatoes
14. Grapefruit
15. Mushrooms

www.foodnews.org

SECTION IV:

CREDITS

1. THE KARP LAW FIRM, P.A., 561-625-1100.
   GUIDE TO VETERANS BENEFITS FOR LONG-TERM CARE EXPENSES GUIDE TO MEDICAID BENEFITS FOR LONG-TERM NURSING CARE COSTS.

2. *MAYO CLINIC ON ALZHEIMER'S DISEASE-YOUR GUIDE TO UNDERSTANDING, TREATING, COPING AND CARE GIVING.*

3. *LIVING THE GOOD LONG LIFE- A PRACTICAL GUIDE TO CARING FOR OURSELF AND OTHERS-* MARTHA STEWART.

4. *MAYO CLINIC GUIDE TO PREVENTING AND TREATING OSTEOPOROSIS.*

5. *YOUR BODY'S MANY CRIES FOR WATER-* F. BATMANGHELIDJ, M.D.

6. *PREVENTION* MAGAZINE.

7. ANITA M. MYERS, UNIVERSITY OF WATERLOO, ONTARIO, CANADA.

8. GORDON COLLEGE CENTER FOR BALANCE AND MOBILITY, WENHAM, MA.

9. ENVIRONMENTAL WORKING GROUP: *DIRTY DOZEN, CLEAN FIFTEEN.*

10. CREMATION PLANNING AND INFORMATION BOOK, NEPTUNE SOCIETY.

11. JANE SANDERS, OUR FRIEND.

12. ATTENDEES AT OUR CLASSES AT THE FIRST PRESBYTERIAN CHURCH IN NORTH PALM BEACH, FLORIDA.

QUOTES FROM ATTENDEES OF "SUDDENLY ALONE" CLASSES

"When I took your class, I never thought it would happen to me—and now I am **SUDDENLY ALONE**."

"I was having frequent migraine headaches, and after I started drinking more water each day, my migraines stopped."

"I would like to review my completed document with my son and make a copy of the templates for him to complete because one never knows when our entire family will need this information."

"Since the class, women are talking at lunch and over the bridge table about their wishes upon death."

"My husband handles all the financial matters. I better learn how to do these things while he's alive and can explain our finances to me."

"We keep putting off writing our wills and creating a trust. We better make an appointment with an Elder Attorney right away."

"We have been working on one template a day, and have only three more templates to go. Then our notebook will be finished. We have been writing in pencil so that we can easily make corrections."

"Husbands, stop doing everything for your wives: You will leave them helpless and they will drive your kids crazy."

"Men, you have to put soap in the dishwasher for it to work!"

"I'm already living alone, but I need to complete the templates so my kids will know my wishes and where I keep things."

"We already had all of this information, but it was scattered all over the house. Now it is in one place."

"Nobody wants to talk about aging and dying, but since it is inevitable, we better plan for it."

"I never thought about pre-need cremation, but I am going to sign up for it now."

Printed in the United States
By Bookmasters